Learning from Differentiation

A review of practice in primary and secondary schools

Penelope Weston
Monica Taylor
Gari Lewis
and
Annette MacDonald

nfer

INVESTOR IN PEOPLE

Published in September 1998
by the National Foundation for Educational Research,
The Mere, Upton Park, Slough, Berkshire SL1 2DQ

ISBN 0 7005 1527 5

CONTENTS

FIGURES IN THE TEXT

TABLES IN THE TEXT

ACKNOWLEDGEMENTS

Many people have contributed to the preparation of this report. First and foremost are the head teachers, staff and pupils of the 'case study' schools who welcomed members of the research team on numerous visits. The staff were generous in giving their time to talk to us, in allowing us to observe their classrooms, providing us with examples of teaching materials, pupils' work and many other relevant documents. Their contribution was central to the whole study and we are most grateful to them. Many other schools helped by completing a questionnaire on differentiation practice, and LEA staff provided another perspective by giving an overview of how differentiation had progressed across their authority; we thank them all for their help. Valuable support was also given to the research team by members of the Advisory Group.

Within the National Foundation for Educational Research (NFER), we are particularly grateful to Pauline Benefield and other colleagues in the Library for their expertise with bibliographical searches and references; and to our project statistician, Ian Schagen and his colleagues for all their invaluable professional and technical support and their continuing commitment to the study over an extended period. We want to thank Sheila Stoney, Head of the Department of Evaluation and Policy Studies, for her unfailing support during the unusually protracted gestation of this report; and Peter Dickson, Deputy Head of the same department, for his helpful and constructive comments on the draft. Clare Hill was most helpful with editorial tasks. Finally we are deeply indebted to our project secretary, Janine Gray, for her unflagging perseverance through numerous drafts and her calm and cheerful professionalism.

1. ABOUT THE STUDY

1.1 Differentiation in the Nineties

In the last few years there has been a surge of concern about and interest in differentiation, reflected in the growing number of national as well as local in-service courses, in special initiatives, handbooks and reports. Why is this, and how are schools responding? These are the key questions underlying the research reported here.

At NFER, we have developed our own interest in the topic over almost ten years. This started with the national evaluation we carried out for the then Department of Education and Science of the Lower Attaining Pupils Programme (LAPP) (Weston, 1988) As the title starkly indicates, this programme was designed to address the needs of a minority, defined by age (14-16) and, negatively, by academic attainment: the target group was those 'for whom the public (GCE/CSE) examination system had not been designed', crudely labelled as the 'bottom 40 per cent'. From the outset, the variety of approaches and philosophies adopted by schools and local education authorities (LEAs) involved in the programme raised fundamental issues about how to raise attainment – the basic aim of the programme. A major and unsurprising conclusion of the first phase of the evaluation was that effective strategies had to start much earlier and apply to all pupils. What we were talking about, it was clear, was a whole-school strategy to make all pupils more effective learners, recognising their diversity of capabilities and needs. In the light of that finding, the product of the final phase of the evaluation was a research-based handbook, *Differentiation in Action* (Stradling and Saunders with Weston, 1991), designed to help schools move in this direction.

Given its origin in the LAPP evaluation, it is not surprising that the argument in *Differentiation in Action* started from the needs of less successful learners in secondary schools, while continually demonstrating that the range of their needs also related, to some extent or at some stage, to all or most pupils, and could only be effectively addressed by strategies which included all pupils and all teachers. The evaluation had made it apparent that schools often coped with the very real challenge of providing for all their pupils through a whole range of practical solutions, which, at the very least, 'contained' the most difficult problems while often masking the extent of underachievement. From this work it seemed clear that there are persistent problems in the management of learning that make it difficult for many schools to address the learning needs of all pupils as effectively as they intend to do. This became the starting point for our further writing about differentiation (Weston, 1992; Stradling and Saunders, 1993).

It was also apparent that, at the start of the nineties, few schools had arrived at a long-term, whole-school strategy that followed pupils through from entry to exit, tracking and assisting their progress within an agreed framework for learning. That issue has become one focus for other related NFER research and development work, which looked at progression in learning after the 1988 Education Reform Act, cross-phase continuity and progression (Lee, Harris and Dickson, 1995; Schagen and Kerr, forthcoming). The NFER has also been at the forefront of developing sophisticated, statistical analyses to help LEAs and schools monitor performance and identify underachievement (Kendall, 1995; Schagen, 1996; Saunders, 1997) in line with recent Government policy initiatives on school improvement and target-setting (GB. DfEE. SEU, 1997; GB. P. H of C, 1997).

Meanwhile there has been a flurry of publications relating to differentiation. These include: surveys of practice from LEAs (e.g. Devon LEA, 1992; Cambridgeshire CC Inspectorate, 1992) and from researchers (e.g. SOED, 1994); subject-based reviews (e.g. in science, Postlethwaite, 1993); many publications from a Special Needs perspective, resource packs from LEAs and teacher groups, of which the Wiltshire pack (Wiltshire Education Support and Training, 1992) is perhaps the most ambitious; and a number of 'how to' handbooks from groups and consultants who are also heavily engaged in INSET delivery around the country (e.g. Dickinson and Wright, 1993; Visser, 1993). More recently, there have been two collections of papers by teachers and academics on differentiation, one relating to the primary school (Bearne, 1996) and one to secondary school practice (Hart, 1996).

In these publications, as in our own earlier work, there is an implicit tension between the aim of helping all pupils and the pressing priority of those with 'special' needs. As a professional goal, most teachers would accept, almost without thinking, that schools should ensure that *all* pupils maximise their potential. This principle has been sharpened in the last decade, from 1985 onwards, and subsequently reinforced through statutory requirements. The specification of the National Curriculum itself, in all its versions, has made learning objectives for all pupils explicit for all subjects and to all teachers. The publication and implementation of the OFSTED framework, building on the HMI tradition of 'learning match' – matching learning and individual needs – has embodied these requirements in criteria against which schools are being judged. Indeed, the stress on the learning needs of all pupils has become even more evident in the latest guidance (GB. OFSTED, 1995a, b, c). Lastly, the school performance tables agenda, with its links to value-added analyses, raising attainment and school improvement, has created a new agenda of public accountability about the attainment of all pupils in an age group.

Despite the focus on whole-school policies, for all pupils, in practice much of the leadership and driving force behind differentiation policies and programmes linked to this new agenda has come from those with training and expertise in special educational needs (SEN), whether at national, LEA or school level. Indeed, much of the material and practical advice on differentiation has come from this source, and it was the *British Journal of Special Education* which probably presented the most sustained set of arguments on the topic (Peter, 1992). The need of schools' for SEN expertise has increased with the implementation of a parallel national initiative on special educational needs, with the introduction of the detailed requirements of the SEN Code of Practice (GB. DfEE, 1994). The need to satisfy the requirements of the Code of Practice has provided further impetus to use SEN professionals' skills to underpin LEA and school policies and practice. While these requirements are not all related to learning, some of them – for example the introduction of Individual Education Plans for children deemed to have SEN – are highly relevant to the wider differentiation debate.

Another outcome of our early discussions on differentiation was a suspicion that there were continuing problems for schools in reaching a consensus about goals, as well as strategies. This was suggested by underlying differences of view about how best to achieve the overall aim of raising attainment for all and, by implication, about the learning potential of pupils, especially those with designated special educational needs. In other words, we suspected that while there were pressures from a number of sources to assume that there was a professional consensus on differentiation, in practice underlying differences and confusions persisted within the teaching community. Thus the debate has focused sometimes on curriculum (should all pupils cover the same or different course content); on pupil outcomes (where differentiation is seen by some as a measure of the differing responses by pupils to a common task or stimulus); or on pedagogy (matching classroom approaches to learning needs). Furthermore, these aspects may be confused. A term such as 'individualised learning' could mean that each pupil was in effect following a different curriculum or that different methods for tackling a common task were encouraged. Expressions often adopted by teachers, such as 'differentiation by input', 'by dialogue' or 'by output', might suggest that these are all

3

valid interpretations of a single principle. In fact, they may be convenient labels used by teachers holding widely differing beliefs about how best to help all children reach their potential. Organisational issues, about ability grouping between or within classes, and the amount of time devoted to whole-class teaching, may in practice be an important component of 'differentiation in practice'.

Given these developments, trends and problems of interpretation, how were schools responding to the increasing demand to ensure that all pupils learned effectively? Was differentiation really a key issue now? And, if so, what did that mean in practice? How were schools applying the ideas and advice offered in handbooks and courses?

1.2   The Project

The aim of this project, therefore, was to return the debate to school level by reviewing how schools themselves were interpreting and implementing differentiation policies, and to investigate how their practice was being related to overall effective learning and raising attainment goals. Are there common understandings and approaches? How far are managers' aims and policies shared and understood by the rest of the staff? What difference does any policy make to classroom practice? And, above all, to the learning experience and achievements of pupils? How context-specific are particular strategies? And is the agenda changing, in response to national initiatives and pronouncements?

The methods used for the project reflect the concern with what actually happens in schools. We wanted to work with schools which are themselves committed to differentiation goals (although the nature of these goals may vary) and are probably recognised by others as being so committed. This did not necessarily mean they provided examples of 'good practice', but simply that they were working on a differentiation initiative. In some schools the initiative might only involve a few teachers, rather than the whole school.

The design of the project aimed to balance breadth and depth in several ways. We wanted to have:

♦   an overview of existing thinking about differentiation;

♦   a national compass;

♦   coverage of primary and secondary phases;

♦   direct evidence from schools and classrooms;

♦   views from pupils, teachers, managers, LEAs.

In order to make the project manageable, we decided to focus on the two middle stages of compulsory schooling, Key Stage 2 and 3. This would allow us to monitor practice as it affected a broad age group – 8-14+ – and to compare the approaches of primary and secondary colleagues. These two stages seemed to offer a good balance: in each, the range of difference in pupil capabilities and measured achievement was known to be wide and the schools had some degree of choice in the way they met this challenge, within the common requirements of the national curriculum framework. We were aware that by looking at Key Stage 2 rather than Key Stage 1 we might miss some of the more innovative practice, but at the same time felt that it would be particularly valuable to review how schools were handling the major challenges posed by the implementation of the national curriculum for Key Stage 2. Focusing on these two stages also kept the issue of progression from one stage, and probably one school, to the next, firmly on the agenda. We also wanted to know about the resources available to schools for such initiatives, particularly from the LEA.

We started with some preliminary visits to schools to clarify current issues. Then, to achieve the balance of breadth and depth, we undertook a telephone survey of 53 LEAs – a random sample, at that time, of almost half the LEAs in England and Wales – to find out how they and the schools in their authorities had been tackling differentiation. From their suggestions, we identified 14 schools across the country which we visited during 1995 – nine on a number of occasions, some only once or twice – to investigate their particular approach to differentiation. The nine case studies included a common programme of interviews with teachers and pupils and lesson observations, but also allowed us to pursue the school's own priorities – for example, using laptop computers to assist pupils' learning, or taking forward a programme to implement differentiation throughout the school with the support of the Learning Support department. During the autumn term of 1995, we undertook a questionnaire survey of a national sample of schools providing for Key Stage 2 and/or Key Stage 3, to test out some of the ideas emerging from the school case studies on this broader and more representative body of teachers. Parallel questionnaires went to head teachers of primary schools with Key Stage 2 pupils and secondary schools with Key Stage 3 pupils; questionnaires covering some of the same issues were sent to heads of English, mathematics and science in the secondary schools. All the figures and tables in the report are based on the responses to that survey, unless otherwise stated. Further details on the case studies and the survey are given in the Appendix.

As with any project, we faced a number of practical and conceptual challenges and we had to adapt our original design to some extent in the light of events. It is important to recognise that it was *not* the purpose of the project to produce 'case studies of good practice' which would tell schools definitively 'how to do it'. Rather, the project has produced a useful body of evidence to review how schools are 'practising' differentiation in a variety of contexts, with varying degrees of apparent impact on classroom practice and the experience and achievements of individual pupils.

Since the case studies and the survey were completed, the public agenda has moved on. In particular the publication of Key Stage 2 results, the increasing focus on school effectiveness through the work of the Department for Education and Employment (DfEE) and OFSTED, the growth of LEA systems to feed back performance data to schools and, most recently, the development of a statutory programme of target setting for schools, (GB. OFSTED, 1996; GB. DfEE. SEU, 1997; GB. P. H of C, 1997, p. 26, para 12) have all contributed to schools' concern – reflecting, policy makers', some might say, obsession – with raising attainment. The search for effective action is perhaps reflected in the widespread appeal and sales of handbooks on 'raising attainment' (e.g. Saunders, Stradling and Gallacher, 1996). However, practice in classrooms does not usually change so fast. This why we hope that we can indeed 'learn from differentiation': that is, we can build on what schools have been saying and doing to plan effective responses to the agenda as it is developing at present. Using this evidence, and the findings of other researchers who have been addressing these issues, it is our aim to draw out implications and suggestions for teachers and managers in schools about school strategies and classroom practices which lead to effective learning as we approach the millennium.

1.3 The Report

The report has been designed to balance issues and findings, in order to take the reader through the debate which, as a research team, we found ourselves engaged in throughout the project. In the next chapter, therefore, we start with a review of the differentiation agenda, as it has emerged in published accounts and as it appeared in our own findings from practitioners in LEAs and schools. As the chapter shows, it is much easier to find agreement on some aspects of that agenda than on others. This is why we felt it was necessary to meet this challenge early on, so that we could set out some criteria and frameworks within which to consider the evidence in later chapters. As one teacher in another study has graphically put it, differentiation 'is like a bar of soap...you try and grasp it and suddenly it shoots out of your hand' (Kershner and Miles, 1996). For this reason, it seems important to set out at this point, as part of the research context, some of the ideas that have in reality emerged at the end of the study, in order to provide signposts for readers, rather than expecting them to have to infer a definition from the evidence. We also outline the framework we developed for the case studies and the survey and introduce the case-study schools and their differing approaches to differentiation, which raise many questions about purposes, strategies, implementation and review.

The bulk of the project evidence is reviewed in the three following chapters which use the evidence from case studies and surveys to address these questions from three complementary school-based perspectives: those of pupils, teachers, managers.

The last chapter draws on the implications of the evidence to suggest what we can indeed learn from differentiation. It discusses the problems and challenges, as well as the achievements, which emerged from the schools with which we worked. If differentiation has proved both a slippery concept and professionally challenging, does this imply that we all just have to keep on trying harder or that – perhaps – some rethinking is needed? This final chapter uses ideas that were already emerging from some of the case-study schools, and which fit easily with the new stress on target-setting, to suggest ways in which professional expertise, developed though the 'differentiation decade', can fuel a more coherent and positively defined programme of effective learning for all pupils.

2. THE DIFFERENTIATION AGENDA

We have established that differentiation has been much discussed by national and local policy makers, and has been the subject of countless inservice training courses and booklets for several years. In this chapter, we want to explore this agenda a little further. Do schools themselves see differentiation as a priority? If so, why is this, in their view? Is there consensus, in public discussion, about what differentiation really means and how it can be put into practice? How do education professionals, in LEAs and schools, translate the ideas and practical recommendations in their own context? The chapter ends with a summary of the position we developed as a result of the early exploratory stage of the study and our previous work – a working model we could use as a basis for investigating practice in schools.

2.1 Differentiation as a Priority for Schools

Survey evidence

The feeling that differentiation is a current priority in schools was borne out strongly by the national survey. Headteachers and their senior managers were asked to compare its priority rating in their overall school policy in that year (1995/96) and three years before. The results are shown in Figure 2.1.

Figure 2.1: Priority given to differentiation by school managers in 1995/6 compared with three years before

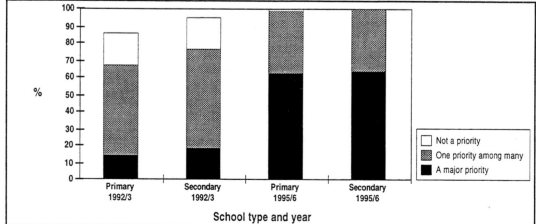

Based on 404 primary schools and 290 secondary schools.
(2 secondary schools and 1 primary school failed to respond to these questions.)
Some respondents (11% of the primary sample, 4% of the secondary sample) felt unable to give a priority rating for 1992/3.

First, ratings for 1995/96 were almost identical for primary and secondary schools: 61 per cent of primary and 63 per cent of secondary senior managers saw differentiation as a major priority in 1995/6; and for almost all the rest it was at least one priority among many. Secondly, the priority rating of differentiation has apparently shot up in the last few years, especially for primary schools: looking back, only 14 per cent of the primary headteachers considered differentiation had been a major priority in 1992/3 and the figure was only slightly higher for secondary schools (19 per cent).

Some case-study evidence

By definition, the case-study schools were chosen because they had already been tackling the issue of differentiation using a variety of approaches and meeting with variable success. Even among these schools the awareness of the importance of differentiation was growing. Some had recently begun monitoring and moderation processes to measure the effects of earlier differentiation policies and practices in their school. Those which had had INSET on differentiation a number of years before were beginning to acknowledge the need for new impetus. One response was to invite outside consultants in to stimulate progress; others made it an integral part of their school development plan (SDP).

♦ Evidence from *Bankside High* showed that differentiation had been developing gradually, from a concept which had traditionally been perceived as threatening or mysterious to teaching staff to one which, it was hoped, would be embraced as the answer to almost all the problems encountered in the classroom, whether it was ensuring equal access to the curriculum for all students, or dealing with behavioural and disciplinary issues at the classroom level.

It was becoming recognised that the process of differentiation was an ongoing and constantly developing dynamic, as some schools explained.

♦ The second 'Global Target' in the School Development Plan of one of the secondary schools (*Headland*) was 'to carry out a self-review of factors which maximise pupils' ability to achieve their full potential'. This target was to be developed and monitored over a period of three years, and involved whole-school INSET on differentiation, and unspecified 'ongoing work on differentiation'. It also included a review of the recently introduced 'more able' policy.

♦ Another secondary, *Lake High,* also had differentiation as an ongoing priority for the whole school, with a salutary comment; 'Each priority must constitute a challenging requirement of all teams on campus – so that each makes [an] explicit contribution towards the priority by specifying targets in its own development plan.' This explicitly put the onus on to the faculties and moves the priority from the Senior Management Team (SMT) towards middle management.

Both of these examples show differentiation as 'one priority among many'. However, this is perhaps not surprising, given their long-term commitment to differentiation in their school.

Why was differentiation a priority?

In the survey, we asked all those who had rated differentiation as a priority of some kind – which meant almost all the respondents – what factors were making it so. The results are shown in Figure 2.2, which gives the percentage of respondents in each phase who considered a factor to be 'very important' in making differentiation a priority and also the percentage seeing a factor as 'not relevant'.

For both phases, the need to 'raise attainment' was seen as a key influence, with half or more of the schools rating it as 'very important' and less than 10 per cent dismissing it as not relevant. But it seemed that this was perceived more as an internal imperative than the result of external pressures. Less than one-third saw OFSTED inspections as a key factor and, even for secondary schools, 'league tables' were not rated as a very important influence on differentiation policy making. Indeed, at this point in time (the end of 1995), a majority of the primary schools (which all catered for Key Stage 2 pupils) saw league tables as irrelevant; it seems likely that such a perception will have changed by now. So if raising attainment was a key motivator for differentiation policy, what was associated with it?

Responses to the other factors point to an interesting underlying story. For primary heads, 'encouraging independent learning' was the most commonly endorsed factor (59 per cent saw it as 'very important'), pointing to an intrinsic professional and pedagogical motivation for their differentiation policy. It was slightly less high profile for secondary schools, but nevertheless 40 per cent saw it as a key influence on their policy. But there were also other more pragmatic factors, which in this type of question only hint at the real underlying issues: these were the nature of the pupil intake and the need to improve pupil behaviour.

Figure 2.2: Factors making differentiation a priority for secondary and primary schools

1. 'Very important' factors

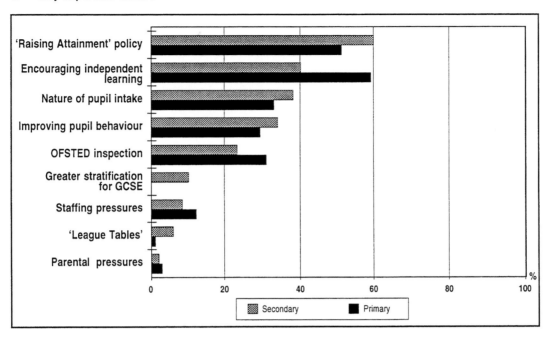

2. 'Not relevant' factors

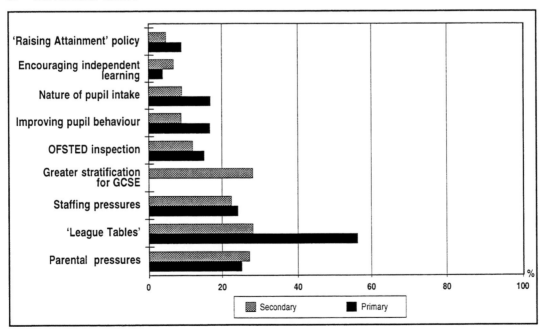

Based on all those who rated differentiation as a current priority:
   392 primary schools, 283 secondary schools.
A series of single response items.

All these factors link differentiation to pupil needs, suggesting that the reason why they were making differentiation a priority was because they perceived a gap to be bridged, between where (many) pupils were and where they should be. If all pupils could be helped to become independent, motivated learners, it suggests, then perhaps their attainment would indeed be raised. Clearly, this is only part of the story – it says nothing about access to the curriculum and the work of teachers – but it does place pupils and their needs at the centre.

For primary school head teachers, the importance of pupil needs in pushing differentiation up the policy agenda was confirmed by further analyses to identify the dimensions underlying the set of responses. Two other themes emerged, both associated with pressure on senior managers: one related to staffing and parental demands, the other with external demands, exemplified by OFSTED inspections. For secondary schools, the underlying dimensions were rather different, suggesting that concern about commitment to learning (linked to pupil motivation and staff morale) was a reason for making differentiation a priority. In these analyses, the significance of 'league tables' was linked to raising attainment as an influence on secondary policy.

It is not surprising that primary and secondary schools seemed to have rather different motivations for making differentiation a priority. As we shall see throughout this report, the thinking of staff in the two phases was coloured by their differing classroom traditions, as well as by the pressures which they felt were affecting what schools did. After all, most primary staff and their head teachers expected to provide for the range of learning needs within their class by varying pace, materials or methods for individuals or groups, at least for some of the day. Pupil learning needs were therefore a natural starting point for the new policy interest in differentiation. By contrast, most secondary teachers – meeting many classes in a day – were more likely to be working against a background of whole-class teaching, perhaps to sets or ability groups of some kind. It was when whole-class teaching was manifestly not working – as indicated by pupil behaviour or staff morale – that pressure for more effective differentiation might seem particularly relevant, especially given the pressure to raise attainment.

What these results suggest is that differentiation had certainly become a key concept for head teachers in both phases, and the reasons for this were a mixture of a positive professional drive to improve learning, a response to external pressures to achieve the same goal and a growing concern, particularly in secondary schools, about the behaviour and performance of a proportion of their pupils.

2.2 The Public Agenda

The reasons which headteachers stated for placing differentiation high on their current policy agenda give us some idea of how and why differentiation fits into their overall priorities. But it is impossible to trace all the influences that have contributed to this perception or to their own particular interpretation of differentiation principles and practice. By reviewing some of the published material on differentiation that has emerged in the last decade and contributed to the debate in INSET meetings and other professional discussions we can form a clearer idea of what lies behind the growing importance which differentiation has acquired.

Dilemmas about differentiation

From the moment when differentiation began to enter the general educational vocabulary, there have been dilemmas and contradictions about its meaning and purpose, as well as about its practical implications for pupils and teachers. At one extreme, it could be described as a particular form of ideological solution to educational problems:

> *Differentiation implies the imposition of different curricula for different groups – or it means nothing.* (Simon, 1985, p. 4)

It might be thought that, a decade after the introduction of GCSE and discussions leading to the introduction of the national curriculum, and several years after the publication of the first OFSTED framework, such concerns would now be a thing of the past. Indeed, by 1992 Susan Hart, whose thinking and writing about differentiation has evolved over this period, was suggesting that a 'new orthodoxy seemed to be fast taking root'. Drawing on HMI reports over the years, she said:

> *The implication ..is that more and better differentiation is what is required: more careful assessment and monitoring of children's needs as individuals, and the development of teachers' skills in providing a learning environment which is sufficiently flexible to allow all children's needs to be taken into account...... In professional discourse, the assumption that differentiation is an essential feature of 'good practice' is increasingly taken for granted, the debate having now turned to how best it might be achieved, given the demands of particular subject disciplines and the human and material resources available to schools.* (Hart, 1992, p.132)

Hart suggested that even when the debate is about pedagogy (rather than about grouping and other organisational strategies), old assumptions which focus attention on the limitations of the individual – rather than the curriculum – easily resurface, suggesting that differentiation is really about making children fit the system rather than – as apparently intended – matching learning tasks to pupils (Hiass, 1990). In taking account of what has been written and recommended about differentiation, therefore, we need to be aware of some of the dilemmas that continue to lurk under the surface of this 'new orthodoxy'.

More recently, in contributions to an edited collection of papers on *Differentiation and the Secondary Curriculum* (1996), Hart has discussed these dilemmas at greater length, explaining her own engagement:

> *I had problems in coming to terms with the emergence of 'differentiation' as a new discourse of 'good practice' because all my thinking about teaching and learning, throughout my professional life, had been developed within a framework which identified 'differentiation' not as a solution but as a major cause of inequality and under-achievement.*

(Hart, 1996, p. 10)

In a useful review of the development of the 'current orthodoxy', through HMI and DES publications in the late 1970s and 1980s, she explains how she revised this view, recognising how their criticism about teachers' lack of differentiation 'was in effect a concern about entitlement and opportunity at all points of the notional ability range'. Her disquiet is about the restriction of inspectors' and policy makers' focus on the 'notional ability range', since the boredom and under-achievement which could be observed in many secondary classrooms – at all 'ability levels' – could be linked with a failure to recognise all the other ways in which pupils differ. Indeed, Hart's professional approach is to see this diversity as a resource which could be used to enhance pupils' active involvement in learning. While recognising that the new orthodoxy is concerned about teaching methods and individual learning needs (rather than 'horses for courses'), she expresses concern about the likely impact of more carefully differentiated assessment and provision to build on existing attainments. How can schools avoid the obvious, and less obvious, constraints and assumptions that in practice limit pupils' potential and demoralise them? In other words, how can differentiation promote, rather than limit, equality of opportunity, which is seen as a fundamental aim for education?

This discussion refers to some of the dilemmas which recur in academic and practitioner debates about differentiation, as it is now understood. Beneath them all rumbles the continuing war of words about the nature of education, and what we really mean when we glibly include in schools' prospectuses those phrases about enabling all children to achieve their potential. To satisfy that aim, what should be common and what different? The underlying tensions have sometimes been described in ideological terms, with differentiation being seen as a denial of equality of opportunity (Simon, 1985); or conversely as a means of realising it; alternatively, differentiation, in the form of different courses, pace or teaching approaches for different groups or individuals, has been seen as appropriate by those who stress relevant, rather than equal, opportunities. The establishment of a national – and therefore common – curriculum has simplified the argument to some extent, since all children are to achieve their potential within this one framework, but it has done little or nothing to resolve the debate about how this might be achieved. It may have been part of the new orthodoxy that differentiation is certainly about pedagogical strategies and not 'just' organisational solutions such as setting or streaming (Stradling *et al., 1991*). But the 1997 White Paper, *Excellence in Schools* (GB. P. H of C, 1997) makes it extremely clear that, at least for older children, the answer is that both are relevant, since meeting individual needs in mixed ability classes is only likely to succeed with excellent teachers.

The apparent dilemmas linked to equality of opportunity are also evident in other recent publications. In a collection of papers on differentiation in the primary school (Bearne, 1996), persistent worries about its meaning and implications run throughout the text. The tension between 'seeking to find differences between pupils' and 'providing equitable access to education for all' is identified at the outset and the editor acknowledges that 'any attempt to unpick the notion of differentiation immediately stumbles into a set of contradictions and tensions'.

Other concerns which relate to fundamental ideas about the nature of teaching and learning also persit in the same book. In this case the tension is more difficult to define, but seems to contrast *precision* (of pupil/task match) with *diversity*. While stressing that the collection presents a range of views, Bearne links differentiation with diversity and 'the assumption that diversity and difference are welcome in classrooms'. This approach apparently widens the agenda very considerably, almost to imply that differentiation is about letting a thousand flowers bloom – encouraging greater diversity in (for example) learning approaches, resources, classroom management methods, methods of assessment, to match the many dimensions of diversity in pupils, relating not only to ability but to gender, personality, learning style and all the variations affecting mood and development at any age. We may contrast this interpretation with highly focused applications of differentiation in practice, in which precise tasks are very carefully matched to specific diagnoses of pupils' capabilities and learning difficulties, for example by SEN specialists, or in a structured, individualised programme (paper or computer-based).

Perhaps the open/structured distinction relates partly to the type of teaching strategy in use. Cooper and McIntyre (1996) present a continuum of teaching strategies which runs from 'transmission', through interactive and reactive, to self-directed learning. The criterion of interest is the degree to which pupils' ideas and knowledge are used to steer the learning process. Thus in 'interactive' teaching, pupils are encouraged to contribute their own ideas so that they can engage more effectively with the main focus, which is a teacher-specified topic or task; whereas in reactive teaching, lesson objectives, content and strategy are determined by the teacher's perception of pupil concerns or interests. While the authors recognise that many teachers combine these approaches, as appropriate, it could be argued that a prevailing empathy with reactive strategies may be linked with support for differentiation as the encouragement of diversity, rather than the precision implied by 'task-matching'. More broadly, it may help us to understand how teachers' practice of differentiation is more likely to reflect their overall teaching strategy and culture than any ideological position or even technical knowledge of differentiation mechanisms and processes. Thus, school phase (primary or secondary; early years or Key Stage 2), subject discipline and level of expertise are just some of the factors likely to influence the way teachers translate overall definitions about differentiation, for example as a 'planned process of intervention in the classroom to maximise potential based on individual needs' (Dickinson and Wright, 1993).

The idea that interpretations of differentiation are coloured by underlying educational outlooks is strengthened by the contrasting views of primary and secondary teachers in the two recent collections of papers. In one contribution (Davidson and Moore, 1996), the difference, and the reason for it, are made explicit. The Year 6 teacher explains that her interpretation:

> *is one which I believe fits in with a child-centred philosophy and is consistent with traditions of primary education as they have evolved in Britain since the Plowden Report [GB. DES, 1967]. It is a pedagogical principle which examines the needs of the child before attempting to provide learning experiences (consistent with statutory requirements) which will best meet those needs and enhance learning.*
>
> (Davidson and Moore, 1996, p.29)

She describes how, within the class, the teacher is both planning (in the light of her in-depth assessment of the need of pupils) and adjusting those plans, in response to children's reactions. Her secondary colleague, working with Year 7 pupils, starts from the subject structure of the secondary curriculum and the organisational constraints of timetabling. Although there is some superficial similarity in the definition of differentiation, in relation to meeting individual needs and raising attainment, it focuses on the work offered, and on the ability dimension: 'providing relevant, stimulating, appropriate and challenging work for all abilities'.

Some writers can see a dilemma about the starting point or focus for differentiation: *differentiating pupils, or curriculum and teaching approaches*. Ironically, as we have seen, many primary teachers see the task as starting from pupils' needs, but 'differentiating pupils' has usually implied sorting them into groups, and focusing mainly on one of the many possible dimensions of difference – conventionally ability or attainment. (In our current system, of course, pupils are – wherever practicable – already grouped on an age criterion.) But many teachers, particularly in primary schools, would argue that pupils differ in so many ways that this approach is at best a very crude solution to meeting individual needs, and at worst runs all the well-established risks of limiting expectations. But focusing on pupils, and pupils' abilities, does not have to imply organisational solutions: those most concerned about equality of opportunity continue to press for the interests of identifiable subgroups of learners with special needs – most obviously the 'low attainers' (for whatever reason) and the 'exceptionally able' (e.g. Eyre, 1992, 1994). In other words, recognising and carefully analysing specific needs has been the starting point for devising effective learning strategies. It is not surprising, therefore, that much of the developmental work on how to put differentiation into practice in 'ordinary' classrooms, and for the whole ability range, has come precisely from those with training and expertise in the field of Special Educational Needs (e.g. Ainscow 1989, 1994, 1998; Peter, 1992; Visser, 1993). Postlethwaite (1993) recognised this contribution and furthermore argued that provision for those with special needs of any kind was actually more effective when implemented by teachers who thought about varied provision for all pupils in their classes.

Postlethwaite was writing about differentiation in relation to science teaching, although much of his thoughtful and persuasive account is relevant to any subject and to most teaching contexts. However, the focus on a specific curriculum area allows him to investigate ideas and approaches which are especially relevant to science. In fact, he demonstrates that the apparent tension between 'differentiating pupils' and 'differentiating the curriculum' is an unreal one. Within the context of a common curriculum, and starting from the assumption that differentiation relates to all pupils, he discusses in considerable detail 'the characteristics of pupils which are relevant to their learning of science', and goes on to suggest tactics which teachers might use to address needs relating to these characteristics, and the ways in these tactics might be brought 'into play in the complex context of a busy laboratory or classroom'. He is able to show the importance of conceptual understanding and the value of error diagnosis in explaining conceptual confusions. A thoroughly practical review of this kind, soundly based on research and appropriate theory, can illustrate how the dilemmas that arise from more generalist discussion of differentiation can, in practice, be resolved. But it also underlines the serious professional challenge that such a teaching programme presents, even for subject specialists working within their own discipline. The sheer scale and complexity of the task is indicated by some LEA guidelines, as in this definition from Essex:

> *Differentiation is the process by which curriculum objectives, teaching methods, assessment methods, resources and learning activities are planned to cater for the needs of individual pupils.*
>
> (Bates and Wolton, 1993, p.6)

It seems, therefore, that underlying dilemmas about differentiation can be usefully defined in more pragmatic terms. In discussing the implications of differentiation for classroom practice, we can identify a tension between the *striving to simplify* and the goal of *managing ever-greater flexibility, diversity and complexity*.

Given this complexity, which makes it apparent that what is under discussion is the whole domain of appropriate pedagogy and the nature of classroom discourse and management, it is scarcely surprising if teachers and writers have sought to tame differentiation by attempting to simplify it (Weston, 1992). A key issue here is that of teacher confidence: handling complexity calls for a level of professional expertise which certainly cannot be expected of the newly qualified or even, perhaps, the 'competent' teacher (NFER, 1997). This confidence may not only be a function of general professional development but also of the task or curriculum content. McGarvey *et al.* (1997), quoting Gross (1993), suggest that primary teachers may have faced a double challenge in recent years, when the more conscious focus on differentiation has coincided with the implementation of the national curriculum:

> *The introduction of the national curriculum initially appears to have decreased teachers' confidence in their ability to adapt tasks and teaching and learning styles to meet the wide range of ability in their classes.*
>
> (Gross, 1993, p. 27)

This can be seen even in the way teachers discuss differentiation. In an interesting exploration with primary teachers, Kershner and Miles (1996) used student teachers' ideas presented on cards as a stimulus. Two very contrasting cards represented these two ends of the spectrum. In each case, some teachers recognised an idea relevant to their classroom approach; either the need to manage diversity by grouping children within the classroom 'by ability' for at least some topics, or – usually for the more experienced teachers – the recognition that meeting individual needs was a complex task which needed continual reflection and development.

Figure 2.3:   Primary teachers' views on differentiation

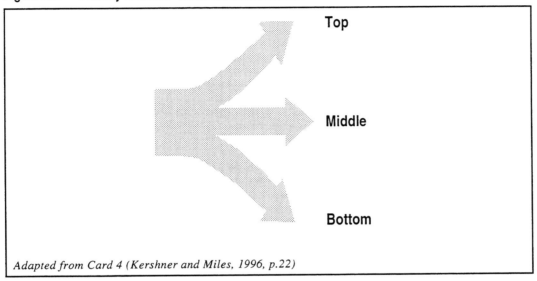

Adapted from Card 4 (Kershner and Miles, 1996, p.22)

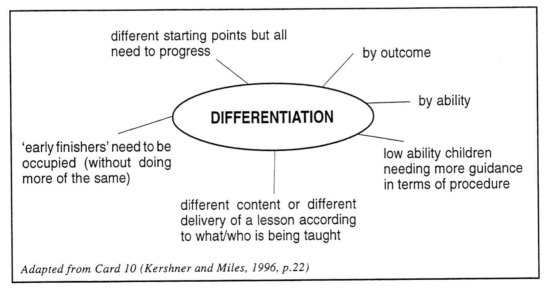

Adapted from Card 10 (Kershner and Miles, 1996, p.22)

The urge to make differentiation more practicable by simplifying the task is therefore both understandable and perhaps appropriate for certain contexts. However, Hall (1997) has nicely encapsulated the problems that may ensue from the best-intentioned plans. She describes how an experiment to introduce differentiation by task in Year 9 science classes in an inner city secondary school, in order to raise attainment, had the opposite effect for the lower ability students, seriously demotivating them. This was the result of using colour-coded work cards which were quickly decoded and rejected by students receiving the lower levels, who resented both the content and the implications of being given them: 'Everyone says we're useless and now you're saying it too.' These effects could have been ignored, given the results of the experiment as a whole, which suggested that, overall, the classes with the differentiated cards did better than the control group, apparently because the middle and higher ability students benefited from the 'higher level' cards.

These continuing concerns and dilemmas reflect practitioners' as well as researchers' thinking about differentiation, which, in turn, influences the already considerable challenge of implementing differentiation strategies. So what guidance is there on how the 'new orthodoxy' can be translated into classroom practice?

Given the underlying influence of HMI thinking on the development of ideas about differentiation, it may be useful to consider the revised OFSTED *Framework for the Inspection of Schools* (GB. OFSTED, 1995d), with its strong emphasis on teaching and learning, to see how principles are now translated into criteria for inspection of classroom practice. Although the term 'differentiation' is not used in the Framework, the differentiation agenda is addressed at many points. There are references in the sections on Attainment and Progress (4.1), Attitudes, Behaviour and Personal Development (4.2), the Curriculum and Assessment (5.2) and Support, Guidance and Pupils' Welfare (5.4). However, the key criteria from Section 5.1 on Teaching seem to be those set out below:

> *Inspectors must evaluate and report on....the quality of teaching and its contribution to pupils' attainment and progress, highlighting.......the extent to which teaching meets the needs of all pupils...*
>
> *Judgements should be based on the extent to which teachers:*
>
> > *...set high expectations so as to challenge pupils and deepen their knowledge and understanding;*
> >
> > *...employ methods and organisational strategies which match curricular objectives and the needs of all pupils;*
> >
> > *...assess pupils' work thoroughly and constructively and use assessments to inform teaching*
> >
> > (GB. OFSTED, 1995d, p.18).

These, and other criteria from the sections mentioned above, provide a challenging agenda, relating to the management of:

♦ assessment policy, targets and evaluation;

♦ curriculum planning linked to assessment information and target-setting;

♦   pupils' motivation and 'learning to learn' capabilities;

♦   equal opportunities and special educational needs;

♦   classroom/pupil/resource organisation;

♦   teaching and learning strategies.

Put like that, it is perhaps not surprising if the single term 'differentiation' proves difficult to break down into operational terms.

2.3   The Practitioners' Agenda

This brief review has already highlighted an issue that will run through this report: the difficulty of translating differentiation into agreed forms of classroom practice. Furthermore, we wish to argue that this difficulty is partly due to the lack of agreement about the underlying concept – about what differentiation really means. However, on the face of it, this was not how it appeared to practitioners in our study when they responded to a direct request for a definition. Even more than we had expected, we found a high degree of consensus in the way it was defined. The LEA respondents – mostly senior inspectors or advisers – were asked to put this in their own words. The consistency of their response is remarkable. The most common definition was based on the idea of addressing or matching individual learning needs – 90 per cent of LEA staff mentioned this as part of their definition. Moreover, just under two-thirds (62 per cent) of the LEA staff we talked to thought this view was shared across their team. Whilst the exact formulation varied, the common focus was clear: as one respondent put it, 'It's an extremely subtle term, but basically it's responding to individual needs.' For example:

> The means by which appropriate provision can be made for all learners within the curriculum framework.

> Differentiation requires the consideration of variables – students, tasks, and learning context – to provide students with the best combination to fully meet their individual needs. This view is prevalent, although the wording may vary.

> Differentiation is the planned provision of learning opportunities to take into account the difference in abilities of pupils in order to ensure they reach their potential.

Other respondents were more cautious about their view, or the extent to which it was shared by schools:

> We are in the throes of getting a definition together.

> Differentiation is the process whereby an *attempt* is made to provide learning experiences which are matched to the needs, capabilities and previous learning of individual pupils.

> We have agreement among ourselves but I'm not sure if it is shared with the schools!

One adviser stressed the continuity of thinking with established primary traditions, referring to:

> the match between learner and task when (a) the learner has sufficient existing knowledge and skill to carry out the task and (b) the task extends the pupil's learning... this is based on Plowden.

Although most inspectors and advisers had been trained as Registered Inspectors by OFSTED, very few thought that the training had directly influenced their thinking on differentiation. As some explained, this was probably because they had already had a well formulated view, but many also felt that the training had not directly addressed the issue. However, a few suggested that using the OFSTED framework as a model and applying it to practice had focused attention on the quality of learning: as one put it, 'OFSTED has pulled it together'. Another spelled this out:

> There's an understanding among the LEA Inspectorate clearly influenced by work done through training for OFSTED inspections, work on classroom observation, looking at the quality of teaching and learning, whether it is matched to ability and extends them.

To gain a complementary perspective, we felt it was just as important to check on what differentiation meant in the schools we visited and in the national survey of schools. In both cases, we tested out the points raised by the public agenda by asking teachers to respond to a set of pre-specified statements, about the *main* focus for differentiation.

Differentiation is MAINLY......

A. Relevant to SEN children

B. About improving teaching methods to suit the task

C. Grouping 'like' pupils together

D. About raising the attainment of all pupils

E. About planning learning to match individual pupils' needs

Teachers interviewed in the case-study schools were asked to pick out which of the statements they felt most strongly about (positively or negatively) and comment on them further. This approach meant that they tended to give their views on only some of the statements, but the pattern of response suggested usefully where teachers' priorities lay. As with the inspectors, the most popular interpretation was that differentiation was to do with 'matching' (Statement E). However, these teachers were also likely to endorse Statement D, which made the reference to 'all' pupils, as well as touching on an underlying goal – raising attainment. Conversely, the only statement provoking disagreement limited the focus of differentiation mainly to pupils with special needs.

> Differentiation is definitely not A. I'd put E first, that's what education is about, extending each child as much as you can. Although it's not always possible, that's what we aim to do. It's also about B, and we're always trying to improve on C and D.
>
> Year 5 teacher, *Observatory Primary*

Another teacher from the same school had a similar view, spelling it out in more detail:

> Differentiation is not A because *all* pupils are different. It could be B, in order to make pupils think. It is C sometimes, when they need pulling together for behaviour and confidence. My aim for each is to go as far as he or she can and to push forward on both their weaknesses and their strengths. I regard E as the altar, the top of Mount Everest, but it's not possible to do every second of every day, so to be realistic differentiation is more likely to be B or D.
>
> Year 4 teacher, *Observatory Primary*

A Special Educational Needs Co-ordinator (SENCO) in a different primary school added other factors:

> My differentiation definition is E mostly, but it's also about raising attainment, pushing the kids a bit all the time, and it's also making sure that the strategy used to differentiate suits the task in hand.
>
> SENCO, *Windmill Primary*

Some secondary teachers also felt strongly that differentiation was for all, but agreed it was complex and indeed should be recognised as a long-term process, as two teachers from *Causeway High* explained:

> As a school we recognise B and D, but we haven't really taken on E; as teachers, we still hold most of the control. We need to work first on improving teaching methods. Then, gradually, as we become more competent, we can hand over more to the children.
>
> Deputy, *Causeway High*

> I disagree strongly with A. It's about B, which may be achieved through C – that's only one way. Differentiation needs to involve a multiplicity of ways. D and E are certainly relevant, but it also raises teachers' awareness of the needs of pupils. Once you've done it and evaluated it, you see the value, you want to do more – I don't think anybody wouldn't..

> SENCO, *Causeway High*

In fact, a number of teachers contrasted the 'ideal' represented by Statement E with the constraints of classroom realities. One saw E as realistic only with 'our bottom band where we have three staff with 15 kids'. Some saw the realistic solution as some form of ability grouping (C); others felt a more radical approach was called for:

> I would aim for differentiation to be about E, although you can't realistically hope to do that for 28 pupils. I aim to do it through grouping and setting (C) and I also see it as D.

> Year 3 teacher, *Abbey Primary*

> Differentiation can be defined in terms of E, D and possibly C – although it is not really grouping because it is to do with the quality of teaching and the expectations of the teacher. It could be B, but not A. But really differentiation is more global. It requires planning, good modules, coherence across time, clearer objectives about what to achieve and how the task and materials can be linked to this.

> Headteacher, *Rock High*

The Learning Development Co-ordinator (SENCO) at *Rock High* explained this in terms of her philosophy:

> Differentiation is D and E/B. Because of my brief as Learning Development Co-ordinator, I see differentiation as essentially concerned with Equal Opportunities. This is the basic philosophy of the LDD. B/E are relevant because planning is essential for classroom and individual learning. They are also relevant because differentiation is about teaching methods and working with teachers to help pupils to learn more effectively.

For one primary head (*Windmill School*) there were also underlying issues, but he was starting from a rather different standpoint:

> Differentiation means being aware of the differences [in children's backgrounds and ability] but being non-judgmental. It is certainly not just an organisational issue, as HMI seem to think. You can plan till the cows come home, but the bottom line is, do the teachers know their children?....[Problems with differentiation] come down to poor observational skills and being unaware that children are struggling.

Other teachers began to explain how definition was worked out in a particular school or subject context:

> I see differentiation as a strategy for raising the attainment of all pupils as an absolute. While many mainstream schools may have a particularly strong need to differentiate downwards, I think special schools are far more likely to need to differentiate upwards. If you're to raise the expectations of pupils you've got to raise the expectations of staff; parents will eventually follow.
>
> Headteacher, 11-16 special school

> In my view half the problem is language skills. The differentiation course we went on recently was liberating because it clarified for me that differentiation is not just about having lots of worksheets. It's both broader and more flexible − about knowing what to expect back from kids. This means you may only need one worksheet − it's more important to use a variety of approaches. If work is always 'materials-led' it becomes very impersonal.
>
> Science teacher, *Hillside High*

> I find differentiation through language the most effective strategy for improving learning; I constantly adjust it as children develop, introducing new terms and reinforcing others.
>
> Science teacher, 11-16 special school

> I believe that English lends itself to mixed ability teaching.. Some can be good speakers and listeners but not writers, or they could have different needs. I think English teachers have a certain attitude to their subject and the teaching of it which means that they are attracted to mixed ability teaching.
>
> English teacher, *Rock High*

Interestingly, it was at a secondary school which had recently changed from mixed ability to much more setting that the head now saw differentiation as a development area:

> I see differentiation as the number one priority; this is the consequence of [re-introducing] setting − of unpicking a quarter of a century of mixed ability teaching. We've found it quite difficult to get our minds round it.

In the national survey, primary and secondary head teachers or senior managers and (secondary) heads of department were asked to respond to the same statements, but in this case they were expected to say how far they agreed or disagreed with each one. As an overview of their response, Figure 2.4 shows the percentage of senior managers in primary and secondary schools 'strongly agreeing' or 'agreeing' with each statement.

The figure confirms the schools' focus on the twin goals of raising attainment and meeting individual needs. In this context, the focus in Statement E is clearly on the conjunction between the curriculum and the individual – the 'match' in learning – and also stresses the importance of planning as an essential element of differentiation. Raising the attainment of all pupils was once again even more important for secondary than for primary teachers. In conversation, and in some questionnaire responses, teachers went out of their way to emphasise that this should apply to *all* pupils.

Figure 2.4: Senior managers' interpretation of differentiation

1. **Primary headteachers' response to statements on differentiation**

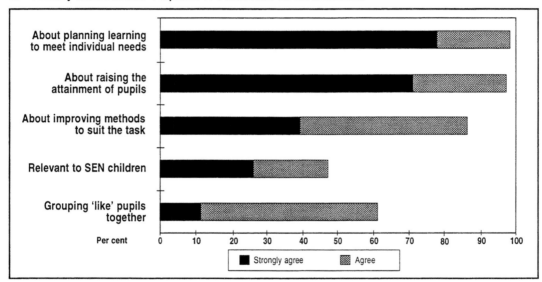

2. **Secondary senior managers' response to statements on differentiation**

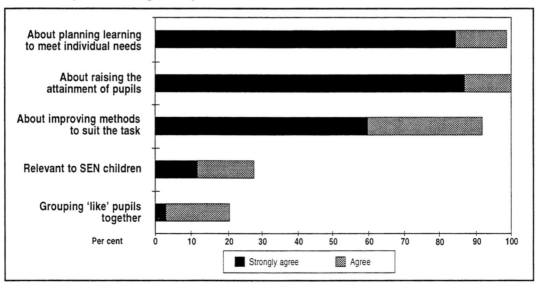

However, within the secondary schools, some heads of department gave interestingly different answers (Figure 2.5). Here the figure shows only the percentage 'strongly agreeing' with each statement.

Figure 2.5:   Heads of departments' interpretation of differentiation

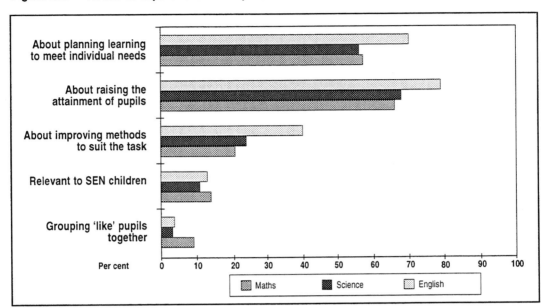

Apparently senior managers in both phases were more inclined to endorse the 'pedagogical' definition (Statement E) than were heads of department. Indeed, only just over half of the heads of maths and science 'strongly agreed' with this statement. Moreover, although 61 per cent of the secondary senior managers were strongly positive about Statement B, on improving teaching methods, this was much less favoured by subject heads, especially the maths and science teachers (for further discussion of this item, see Chapter 5). Indeed, looking at the responses from all three groups of heads of department, the only statement drawing strong support from at least two-thirds in each subject was D, that differentiation was *mainly* about raising the attainment of all pupils.

What seems to be emerging so far from the survey results, therefore, is a strong consensus on principles relating to entitlement: the right of all pupils to have equal access to the curriculum and to the opportunity to achieve. Moreover, the consensus seems to hold across most areas of the country, across LEA and school staff, and across both school phases. For such a 'subtle term', and one which has been used in other contexts with widely differing meanings, this is a surprising outcome. Perhaps it reflects a longer-term consensus about the goal of meeting individual needs, to which 'differentiation' has now been attached as a convenient label. Certainly, the relative lack of emphasis given in the survey to Statement C, identifying differentiation *mainly* with pupil grouping, suggests that the concept was being associated in principle with the teaching and learning process *within* the classroom, and that organisational strategies, such as setting, were not sufficient in themselves as a differentiation strategy.

Further analyses to identify underlying patterns showed that for all groups there were two main dimensions of meaning which were distinguished: differentiation could be related either to pupil categorisation (SEN pupils, pupil grouping) or to raising attainment and individual needs, for all pupils. Interestingly, statement B, on teaching methods, was not really linked with this second dimension.

From investigating practitioners' views on differentiation, we have learned that there was widespread support in principle for the 'new orthodoxy', which assumes differentiation is about enabling all pupils to access the curriculum and maximise their achievement through teaching designed to meet their individual needs. But even at the level of principle, important differences of emphasis emerge, between primary and secondary teachers, between senior and middle managers and between subject specialists. These differences may suggest that some of the long-standing dilemmas about differentiation are still influencing what teachers think, and even more importantly, affecting what they do, in the classroom and in supporting differentiation strategy as managers.

Against this context, we set out the position which was formulated in the first stages of the study to use as a basis for investigations in schools.

2.4   The Research Agenda

Differentiation and learning: a provisional framework

The aim of the research was to find out how those in schools were interpreting differentiation, not to define or advocate our own interpretation. However, we found it essential to develop our own understanding, not least because there were a number of researchers working on the study over time. It would also be disingenuous to say we had no view. Above all, we needed to have some yardstick which we could use in evaluating what teachers and others said about differentiation.

What we sought was not a watertight definition – a fruitless quest – but a working model of how differentiation may influence and shape pedagogy: the process of teaching and learning in the classroom. We acknowledged that the organisational dimension, represented by setting, banding and other ways of grouping pupils by ability or aptitude, was an important aspect of differentiation practice and would need to be investigated, but we also accepted the common view that, even classes grouped in this way are far from homogeneous. We therefore wanted a way of thinking about differentiation as a pedagogical strategy (Stradling *et al.*, 1991), intended to help individual pupils not only to access the curriculum but to improve on their previous best. The guidelines set out by Bates and Wolton for Essex LEA in 1993 express the aspiration well:

> *The purpose of differentiation is to enable every individual to reach the highest possible standard of which he or she is capable. Differentiation expands the possibility for individual achievement rather than diminishing the task to a pre-conceived level of individual ability* (p.6).

This was, of course, written for the 'real world', within a set of guidelines for secondary schools for effective differentiation in the classroom. However, from our early exploratory visits to schools, it was evident that it remained largely an aspiration. Pressure to cover the National Curriculum programmes of study, assumptions that in practice the main thrust of differentiation was help for the less able (and in a few cases the most able as well) and, above all, the feeling that differentiation posed an impossible challenge for teachers, all conspired to suggest that differentiation was not a practical proposition in most classrooms. We therefore felt we needed a model which put classroom practice at the centre, but took account of the roles – or potential roles of all the main groups of participants and allowed for diversity in all its aspects. We set these ideas out below.

Within the *unique* context of each school, professionals have the task of balancing the *common* goals of the national curriculum and the *diverse* capabilities and concerns of all their pupils, using the *differing* professional insights and approaches of staff. Differentiation policy and practice can, in these terms, be related to the perspectives of pupils, teachers and managers.

The idea of pupils, teachers and managers as complementary players in effective learning is set out graphically in Figure 2.6.

Its aim is to suggest that the process is more dynamic than the term differentiation sometimes tends to suggest, involving the interaction of task, pupils and teacher. Not everything depends, or should depend on the teacher, however central the teaching role. What differentiation means in practice will always relate to the nature of the task (clearly it is irrelevant to some activities or situations, and the approach will rightly vary from one task to another and according to the stage in a topic or unit). What may be less widely accepted is that the pupils' role in the success of differentiation strategies could probably be much more active than it often seems to be. Do pupils know what the learning targets are for a lesson or topic? Or how these relate to what they have done or achieved before, as a class or individually? What difference does it make if targets are explicit? Does differentiation have to be 'done to' pupils? Nor is the classroom a closed system, since pupils (and teachers) experience many different classrooms, and all those experiences are likely to influence their perceptions and behaviour. Moreover, senior and middle managers may have a considerable impact, for good or ill, on what takes place there, not only by decisions about pupil grouping and resources but by the way they lead school development planning and review.

Figure 2.6: Pupils, teachers and managers: complementary roles in effective learning

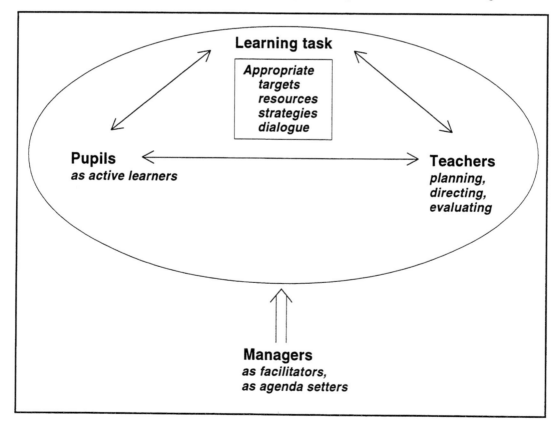

Differentiation practice in the classroom, and its impact on learning performance, we suggest, therefore depends on the role and importance given to each of the participant groups – pupils, teachers and managers – and the way in which the three roles interact.

During the first exploratory phase of the research, we used these ideas to develop a practical framework for the investigation. We devised a *common approach* to explore schools' practice, while recognising the *diversity* which we expected and found in school contexts and traditions. The framework of issues is then presented as it relates to the differing *perspectives* of the main participants – pupils, classroom teachers and managers – whose concerns form the focus respectively of the following three chapters.

Framing a common approach

As we have seen, one of the problems of investigating differentiation is that it is in practice a 'slippery concept', particularly when taken across subjects and phases. Using a common approach and framework, particularly in the first phase of the case-study programme, and again towards the end of the project in the national survey, seemed a useful way of identifying differences, in interpretation and practice, which seemed to be related to the diversity of school settings, and – within these – to contrasts between subjects. By asking broadly the same set of initial questions and adopting the same set of procedures for all the case-study schools, we hoped to have a sound basis for testing emerging ideas about differentiation practice in these diverse contexts and the factors affecting it. For the final stage of the case-study work, we could then pursue school-specific initiatives and ideas in more depth; and we could further test our findings by presenting them to a national sample of primary and secondary schools in the questionnaire survey.

Implementing a common approach meant drawing up a common programme of activities in all the case-study schools. To build up a picture of classroom practice, this meant: observing lessons (mostly in the core subjects); recording teachers' strategies and pupils' activities; and discussing with some pupils and teachers from each of these classes and schools how they understood and practised relevant teaching and learning methods. For the school as a whole, and for departments or other mid-level structures, the collection of relevant policy documents and – where appropriate – attendance at meetings complemented information and perceptions obtained in interviews with middle and senior managers with responsibility for learning policy. The common questions and issues relating to differentiation that were being asked are summarised in Figure 2.7. These were designed to explore participants' knowledge and understanding of activities, structures and processes, either explicitly defined (by school staff) as aspects of their differentiation strategy, or (which seemed to meet the 'orthodox' and widely endorsed interpretation of differentiation), focusing on the match of work to meet individual pupils' learning needs and targets. They covered topics relevant to classroom practice and to the management of learning, at departmental/year group and whole-school levels.

Figure 2.7   Issues and questions included in the common approach

Interpretations *To be explored with all adult interviewees*

What does differentiation mean?

What is the school's policy?

Is it a priority in the school and, if so, why?

How does differentiation relate to equal opportunities, SEN, raising attainment, assessment, target-setting?

Planning learning to match individual needs

What criteria are used as the basis for differentiation – overall ability, specific skills, behaviour/motivation, learning style, etc.

Are individual needs assessed, and, if so, how? Do pupils themselves take part?

Are targets set for individuals? If so, for all or for some (who)? Do pupils know what the targets are, or help to set them? How specific are they?

Do the assessments feed into lesson/curriculum planning, and, if so, how?

How is learning planned – how much is decided at departmental/team level, at class level? What contribution is made by Learning Support staff at the planning stage?

Selecting appropriate strategies

What methods do teachers use to differentiate, within the classroom?

Do they, for example

• set different tasks for different classes/groups/individuals?

• provide materials at different levels?

• encourage pupils to respond in varied ways – written/oral, role play?

• structure pair/group work according to individual need/ability?

• use other adults (or pupils) to support those who need it?

• vary the pace for individuals/groups?

How much responsibility do pupils have in managing their learning? Over what aspects? Is choice of activity a strategy or a reward?

Impact of differentiation

How do teachers know whether these or other strategies are effective?

What do pupils think helps them to learn?

INSET

How much, if any, INSET relevant to differentiation has there been? For whom? What form did it take?

Senior/middle management

What are the **class grouping mechanisms** for Key Stage 2 and 3 and the criteria on which they are based?

Check out aspects of senior/middle management which may intentionally or unintentionally affect differentiation. These include:

♦ **Assessment and recording policy.** How is performance moderated? Is there a common assessment policy? If so, what are the criteria? How is it implemented and monitored? What role if any do pupils play (self-assessment)? How accessible are individual records? How are they used, e.g. to evaluate teaching?

♦ **Academic/pastoral structure.** Are these separate? Who is responsible for a child's overall learning experience and performance – within the school year and across years?

♦ **Staff development and appraisal.** Are these linked to SDP targets related to teaching and learning? Who, if anyone, observes teachers? Are there explicit strategies for continually improving/updating teaching expertise?

♦ **SEN structure.** What does the organisation and staffing of SEN say about improving individual learning? How is it staffed? What clout does the SENCO have? Are there mechanisms to facilitate SEN staff providing professional support for other staff (e.g. structured links to departments, time for observation etc.)?

♦ **Resourcing policy.** Is there a policy linked to learning aims – e.g. use of a resources centre, IT provision and access, – or is it just devolved mechanistically on some departmental/age group formula?

♦ **Subject-specific policy.** It is likely that differentiation approaches will be influenced by the demands of the subject, e.g. communicative competence in modern foreign languages, development of scientific concepts, or subject-related technical skills? Are the subject depts/co-ordinators aware of this? If so, what actions have been taken to address the needs?

♦ **School Development Plan.** How does differentiation feature in the plan? Are there specific targets? Is it 'owned' by the staff?

In the second phase of the case studies, school-specific initiatives and ideas were studied in more detail, thus complementing the common approach with examples of strategies which managers and teachers had developed to fit that school's particular circumstances or stage of development. Finally, all the findings and hypotheses that were emerging from the case studies were reviewed in order to select topics to investigate further in the national survey.

Diversity at school level

So far we have assumed, in general and along with a number of writers on differentiation, that we are discussing a common set of principles and procedures, applicable to any educational context. Is this true? We felt it was realistic to assume that what took place in practice, filtered through professional and school-based cultures and contexts, would probably be very diverse.

For the purposes of the research, school diversity had two aspects. First, we were clear from the outset that we wanted to make comparisons between primary and secondary approaches to differentiation. We imagined that, even in the era of the National Curriculum, the differing traditions of teaching and learning, as well as of class organisation and – usually – school size, would lead to a number of practical differences in what counted as successful differentiation in the classroom. Secondly, we felt that each school's particular circumstances – its context, human and material resources, recent history and leadership, ethos and goals – were likely to influence differentiation priorities and practice.

It also proved convenient to review these school differences under two headings. First, there were the differences in *context*, that is the circumstances in which the school operated and over which the managers had only limited control, such as the nature and size of the pupil intake, staff expertise and resourcing levels, and the school's place within the community. Secondly, there were planned differences in *ethos* and in *policy* relevant to differentiation, particularly at senior level. These differences in context or policy might both have been the catalysts for implementing a differentiation strategy in the first place, and might also have had an influence on the way it was implemented. Some examples of the differences that were identified among our case-study schools are given.

School context. Sometimes the *nature of the pupil population* seemed to set the agenda:

♦ One case-study secondary school (*Hillside High*) faced major challenges affecting the attainment of the school. It served a large, very deprived council estate where the majority of families were caught up in second – or even third-generation unemployment. A significant number of pupils arrived from their primary schools with no reading capability whatsoever. The head and his senior colleagues considered a policy of differentiation the only way forward in breaking out of the cycle of non-achievement and low self-esteem. (The strategies used to instigate a differentiation policy will be discussed in later chapters and reviewed in Chapter 6.)

♦ Another school (*Causeway High*) had a very diverse school population, with a number of non-English speaking refugees and some highly able and articulate pupils whose parents were committed to the school. The school had to be creative in order to provide equality of access to the National Curriculum, and raising attainment at A level was an equally important priority.

Being a small school could also provide a catalyst for a particular approach to differentiation :

♦ *Cottage Primary* was a small, rural school with two mixed-age classes, which created many challenges in terms of ensuring access to the curriculum. As a result of the small numbers, and the fact that there were only two full-time teaching staff, there was an urgency about developing a working strategy for differentiation. The headteacher, who taught one of the classes, had a deep commitment to classroom practices which she felt facilitated effective learning. Differentiation was not in itself explicitly referred to in any of the documentation, as the highly organised strategy was not specifically defined as differentiation, and was already solidly in place.

For other, larger, primary schools the issue was not so much overall pupil numbers but an increase in class sizes, and heads were citing this as a major catalyst in introducing a formal differentiation strategy in the school.

On the other hand, there were clearly contextual factors other than pupil numbers and school size influencing a school's approach to differentiation. One of these was the school's own *history*. In *Rock High,* where the head had been in post for five years, the school had previously been seen as a 'sink' school, at risk of closure. By the time we visited it, the focus on development at every level had enabled the school to become the first in the area to receive an Investors in People award, and an entitlement approach to differentiation had become written into every aspect of the school's planning.

School policy. The importance of *in-school* factors was illustrated by three schools, a secondary and two primaries with similar contexts (in that they served the same local population) and with a good record of partnership, which were found to differ in their differentiation rationale and approach. Two of the primary schools served as feeder schools to *Lake High*, and provided the opportunity for an interesting insight into the approaches taken by the two sectors, given constant characteristics in the intake. The schools had close pastoral links, and in planning transfer to Year 7 the secondary school made good use of recommendations from the primary schools on friendship groupings or children with special educational needs. The schools also maintained somewhat nominal links through a local Heads Forum (collaboration on INSET had ceased some years before due to the perceived differing needs of the schools). Despite this shared background, the three schools all had slightly different, apparently independent, approaches to differentiation.

♦ *Lighthouse Primary* had an approach to differentiation which was quite strongly headteacher-led, and was explicitly portrayed in the Staff Development Plan and in the planned production of a differentiation policy. The main thrust of the differentiation strategy was to ensure that there were three levels of planning for each year group, but there were related policies, such as the 'autonomy policy', which aimed to instil in pupils a sense of responsibility for their own learning. This was done in a number of ways, the most obvious was by regulating the organisation of resource areas so that pupils had the confidence to access their own resources as and when they needed them. The school operated a system of setting for English and Maths.

♦ *Windmill Primary's* differentiation strategy was developed primarily through dissemination of the expertise developed by the SENCO. There was no explicit discussion of differentiation in the School Aims document or in the SDP, although it was alluded to briefly in both of these documents, and it was mentioned in both the science and maths policies. There was no guidance on differentiation specifically from senior management, although they were currently involved in an audit of classroom practice with differentiation in mind. The main thrust of differentiation at this school was its perceived relationship to school ethos. Setting in English and maths had recently begun in this school too.

♦ *Lake High's* approach to differentiation was much more systematised. The school had made it a priority in the SDP, and signalled a large commitment to it by designating two members of staff to co-ordinate the development of differentiation across the school. Individual departments also had a specific mandate to develop differentiation strategies within their own departments; some had progressed with this more than others. Having previously been committed to mixed ability teaching, the school was now moving more and more towards setting by ability, especially in modern languages, maths and science. More recently, the senior management in the school had begun a series of classroom observations as a monitoring exercise, to see how far they had got with differentiation.

It is true that all three schools were characterised by a movement, quite independently, towards more grouping by ability. However, there were primary/secondary contrasts which seemed largely to reflect the more strongly structured systems approach which a secondary school of this size and complexity felt was needed to embed the initiative throughout the institution. One of the primaries also led 'from the top', while the other relied on permeation of relevant expertise through the support provided by the SENCO. As we shall find when we explore management policies and styles in Chapter 5, these differences in style, aims and the expertise of staff as change agents were at least as influential as external circumstances in shaping the school's approach to differentiation.

As we explore classroom practice across these and the other case-study schools in the next two chapters, it will be important to consider how far these differences in school context and policy affected how teachers and pupils worked in the classroom and the way in which teachers attempted to meet individual learning needs. It can already be seen that some of these schools had particular approaches or goals which either made their differentiation policy or practice distinctive, or proved to be at an interesting stage of development. For these schools, later visits were used to pursue these aspects in particular. These investigations included the management of transfer at eleven in the family of schools discussed above and its implications for differentiation and progression; the use of Learning Support departments in two secondary schools (*Rock* and *River*) as the driving force for the whole-school differentiation strategy; the development of laptop computers as a tool for individual learners at *Observatory Primary* school; and the development of pupils' competence as managers of their own learning, from Key Stage 1 onwards, in *Cottage Primary*.

Investigating three perspectives on differentiation

Within each school, we wanted to explore practice from the three complementary perspectives (as indicated earlier, especially in Figure 2.6) of pupils, teachers (as classroom practitioners) and managers (who are of course also teachers). In each case, we wanted if possible to combine practice and perceptions.

Pupils. We wanted to make sure that the pupils' perspective was represented, because of our growing interest in the role which pupils can themselves play in managing their learning. The part played by pupils, in identifying what they already know, understand and can do, how they need to progress and what they think are the most effective means for doing so, has been neglected in much of the debate on differentiation. Given the overall design of this study, we recognised that, methodologically the pupils' perspective would not be a major focus. But we identified certain pupils on whom to focus during lesson observations, interviewed 39 pupils and asked teachers to provide formal and informal assessments of them. Naturally, we were not trying to ask pupils directly about differentiation but, using the issues in Figure 2.7, we wanted to know how they felt their learning needs were being met, what they actually did during lessons and how they interpreted the assessments that teachers made of them.

Teachers. In exploring the teachers' perspective, we looked at all the issues in the left-hand column of Figure 2.7, mostly through interviews but also in lesson observations. Here we want to focus especially on the attempt to identify the strategies or mechanisms which teachers use to implement their differentiation aims in the classroom. This attempt was carried through all three data collection modes: lesson observation, interviews and survey. These different types of evidence throw light on what teachers appeared (to an observer) to be doing; and how they themselves interpreted their actions and priorities, both in discussion (the interview) and in the structured context of formal self-evaluation in the survey.

In looking for a way of categorising differentiation practice in the classroom we rejected classifications into differentiation by task, resource, outcome and so on. While these may be useful analytically, they do not provide a ready way of categorising what teachers and pupils actually do. Starting from the assumption that what teachers wished to do was to enable all their pupils to achieve the best outcome from the planned curriculum, we devised a rather more empirical schema, which is presented in Figure 2.8.

We used this schema to provide an analytic summary of our more detailed lesson observation notes, in which we kept a record both of teacher activities and what a small number of targeted pupils were doing. It tries to capture a wide variety of methods which teachers may use in their endeavour to match curriculum plans and delivery to what individual learners can do. It is a descriptive rather than an evaluative framework, aiming to categorise how teachers actually work with pupils in their classes.

Figure 2.8   Differentiation in the classroom: observation schema

MECHANISM	Practice	How does it promote differentiation?
LEARNING STRUCTURE: COMMON OR VARIED?		
Main lesson task Core and extension	C/V	
Pupil materials Textbooks, stimulus Worksheets/cards	C/V	
Pupil targets/approach how to respond: style, specific task	C/V	
Response mode e.g. written, oral, drawing....	C/V	
Homework	C/V	
RESOURCES: ACCESS TO A *RANGE* OF *(i.e. pupils can use or be asked to use different things)*		
Information resources Books, extracts, databases etc.	Y/N	
Technology resources Computers, tools, apparatus	Y/N	
PUPIL MANAGEMENT		
In-class pupil grouping Groups, pairs, etc.	Y/N	
Increased pupil responsibility Study skills, manage own learning	Y/N	
WORKLOAD/PACE		
Planned variation in time or task	Y/N	
Unplanned differences i.e. some finish 'early'	Y/N	
Planned 'lockstep' all made to finish together	Y/N	
TEACHER-PUPIL INTERACTION		
Individual/small group review/tutorial helping pupils to think and take responsibility	Y/N	
Flexible questioning targeting questions to individuals	Y/N	
Flexible relationships adapting to individuals' needs/capabilities	Y/N	
OTHER INTERACTIONS		
Pupil-pupil interaction Peer tutoring, specified roles	Y/N	
AoTs and pupils Learning support	Y/N	
DIAGNOSTIC ASSESSMENT *any evidence that learning plan is related to/uses*		
Profile *(what pupils know/understand/can do)*	Y/N	
Prior/home experience *(what they can contribute)*	Y/N	
Self-assessment	Y/N	

In interviews, teachers were asked to describe the mechanisms which they found to be the most effective in promoting differentiation. They were shown a list of possible classroom strategies taken from the schema:

♦ planning a common topic/task with a variety of learning materials, differing learning targets or differing response modes;

♦ planning different topics/tasks for some pupils;

♦ varying pupil roles (e.g. presenting, tutoring evaluating);

♦ responding flexibly to pupils' learning needs;

♦ setting and reviewing learning targets individually;

♦ using assessments to plan individual targets.

The survey respondents (primary heads and secondary heads of core subjects) were also presented with this list and asked whether they used the strategies in their teaching of Key Stage 2 or Key Stage 3 classes and, if so, whether they found them practicable.

Evidence relating to these classroom strategies forms the bulk of Chapter 4 on the teachers' perspective.

The purpose of all these inquiries into classroom practice was to understand a little better not only what the teachers were doing, under the heading of differentiation, but why they chose to use certain strategies. To what extent did they feel they had the opportunity (or indeed the resources or expertise) to implement differentiation, as they understood it?

The issues underlying our inquiries with teachers are summarised in Figure 2.9. This brings together pupil and teacher inputs into classroom learning, as they affect the tailoring of schemes of work to the capacities of all the pupils in any particular year group or class. The questions relate to individual teachers and to teams or departments, and in some cases refer to arrangements made by senior managers. In other words, the list of issues assumes that what teachers do is influenced and, hopefully, underpinned by a strategy for learning for which senior managers take responsibility.

Figure 2.9:   Classroom learning and differentiation: issues and questions

---

What are the strategies (if any) for the following, and how are they used?:

♦ diagnosing what pupils know, understand and can do?
are they common to *all* teachers? to sub-groups (e.g. department)?
are they made explicit to pupils? Do pupils contribute?

♦ planning schemes of work or lessons in the light of pupils' capabilities?
are these 'typical' (top/middle/bottom) or actual diagnoses?
what part do teachers play in planning?

♦ using specialist skills at the planning stage (e.g. for materials or methods)
is this a regular practice, or *ad hoc*?

♦ varying the learning mode or materials in the light of:
the demands of the task?
individual capabilities?

♦ enhancing and applying pupils' skills as presenters, peer tutors, team workers?

♦ grouping pupils into or within classes, on the basis of:
general ability/literacy?
skills/knowledge relevant to the task/subject?

♦ providing in-class support
from teachers or learning support assistants?
from other pupils?
from other adults (e.g. parents)?

♦ managing pace and workload within the classroom?

♦ evaluating whether the selected mechanisms have improved performance:
for all pupils?
for pupils with particular needs?

♦ assessing whether the effects were intended or unintended?

Managers.   It has been argued (Qualter, MacGuigan and Russell, 1995) that:

> *differentiation is in practice almost exclusively in the hands of the individual teacher in the classroom. The systems within which that teacher operates may support or hinder the ability of the teacher to differentiate* (p. 151).

While recognising the importance of what takes place in the classroom we would attribute more importance to the managers' role, in planning and leading an effective differentiation strategy for the school as a whole; or, conversely, in constraining what individual teachers can achieve. For this reason, we investigated all the aspects of learning and assessment policy that seemed relevant to our understanding of differentiation, pursuing the questions and issues in the right-hand column of Figure 2.7 in case-study schools through interviews with senior and middle managers, analysis of documents and attendance at meetings.

We were pursuing four underlying questions:

♦ What is the school's intended/actual learning policy?
  (e.g. on core skills, SEN, integration of assessment in learning)

♦ What are the *de facto* indicators for differentiation in the school?
  (Is the real emphasis on setting, special provision for the less able?)

♦ What is the organisational infrastructure to support differentiation?
  (Who is responsible? How is it planned and monitored?)

♦ What is the professional infrastructure to support differentiation?
  (INSET? Use of SEN staff? Appraisal? Observation?)

There was an important additional source of evidence on the managers' perspective, because the national survey was targeted at senior and (in secondary schools) middle managers (heads of department). The questions included in the survey were designed to pursue issues which had been identified in the case-study schools, in order to test their relevance and significance on this much larger and nationally representative sample of primary and secondary schools with pupils in the two selected key stages (Key Stage 2 and 3). In addition to the questions about the priority they were giving to differentiation and their definitions of it, there were three broad management themes in the questionnaire:

Investment/commitment. What evidence was there that the school was formally committed to a whole-school strategy for differentiation, through its SDP and policy documents? What investment had been made, for example, in the form of staff responsibilities or allowances, or in INSET provision or other forms of professional development, to support the strategy?

Structures and systems. What whole-school structures and systems were there to support the planning, delivery and monitoring of differentiation, at senior and middle manager level?

Influences on differentiation. What factors seemed most relevant to a successful differentiation strategy? What seemed to promote or constrain its development in their school?

The managers' perspective is considered mainly in Chapter 5, but management-related issues are highly relevant to differentiation in practice, seen from teacher and pupil perspectives, that is reviewed in the next two chapters.

It must be recognised that our own understanding of differentiation, in principle and in practice, was evolving and changing as we worked in and with schools. We have set out here some of the analytic frameworks which we used during the study. However, the questionnaire, which came near the end of the study, was intentionally influenced by what we had learned from the case studies, and some of the issues and questions arise from our subsequent analysis of all the evidence. In Chapter 6 we shall return to these issues and concepts, as we reflect on the practice we found.

3. MAKING PROGRESS?
PUPILS' PERSPECTIVES ON LEARNING

In reading some of the literature on differentiation, one might be forgiven for inferring that pupils have little active role to play, since so much seems to depend on the teacher's professional expertise in diagnosis, target-setting and planning appropriate learning strategies. However, such an inference would be at odds with professional advice on the pupils' role in the learning process. Comments from our survey of LEA inspectors/advisers indicated that pupils were more likely to be successful learners if they:

♦ were made aware of the purposes of learning;

♦ were encouraged to make judgements for themselves;

♦ were expected to share in assessing their work;

♦ were expected to make choices;

♦ were given opportunities to be 'experts'.

In other words, these professionals were arguing that pupils can make a positive contribution to the process of matching individual needs and learning experiences, which, as we have seen, is felt by most practitioners to be at the heart of the differentiation process. By sharing actively in the process of diagnosis, decision and evaluation, rather than accepting decisions, instructions and assessments made for them and about them, they may actually become more successful. This principle of 'learning to learn', and the steps taken to promote independence, self-management and self-appraisal, were mentioned in many primary schools. One case-study secondary school saw learning development as a key principle of managing teaching and learning:

> At Rock High, we value all pupils and aim to develop their strengths, in all curriculum areas and in a full range of extra-curricular activities, and would equally aim to support and overcome individual weaknesses so that our pupils may move towards becoming independent learners and see learning as a lifelong activity.

In this chapter we examine whether these aims and claims – elaborated further in Chapter 4 and 5 on teachers and school management – match with pupils' perceptions. We consider the following questions:

♦ Do pupils see themselves as enabled and empowered to learn?

♦ Do they feel involved in diagnosis of their needs and review of performance and informed about their progress?

♦ In lessons are pupils aware of the objectives of the work and their targets?

♦ When getting on with work do pupils see themselves as having choices about how they work and with whom?

♦ What sort of help is available to them?

♦ What do they see as helping them most to learn?

We do this by drawing on interview data with 39 pupils (23 primary and 16 secondary), observations of lessons including these pupils in five primary and four secondary schools and, in 20 cases, complementary pupil assessments. Some information on these pupils is given in Table 3.1.

Table 3.1: Information on pupils interviewed about their learning

		Year 3/4	*Year 6*	*Year 7*	*Year 9*
Gender					
	Girls	4	6	3	3
	Boys	7	6	3	7
Ability level					
(Judged by the school)					
	Higher	4	4	2	2
	Middle	4	5	2	4
	Lower	3	3	2	4
	N =	11	12	6	10

Before looking in more detail at the kind of answers pupils gave to the questions outlined above, we can get a glimpse of some of these pupils at work, during lessons that were observed. The aim of these observations was to see how the identified pupils responded during the session to the activities that the teacher expected him or her to undertake.

At *Observatory Primary* school, Mr X's Year 4 class were halfway through their morning, with some pupils working on maths and others on English. The classroom (33 pupils) was crowded and busy. This class had a number of laptops for pupils to use (and to take home), and this made movement more difficult since they were plugged in to the mains. The English work followed up a visit to a local art gallery, and pupils were drafting poems, some of them choosing to use the laptops for this purpose. Mr X had 6 pupils together, going over their maths work, which involved number patterns. John (lower ability) was working on the patterns at his table, and explained to Alan (average ability) what to do, since Alan had missed the teacher's explanation! As Mr X moved around, helping with laptops and checking on progress, Alan and Ned enthusiastically explored possibilities for pattern-making on their laptop. They take it in turns to take it home each day. Then Steve used the spell check and word count, while Julie, still getting used to the laptop, followed through a 'turtle walk' to create a drawing. After half an hour, Mr X brought the class together to talk about the English work pupils had been doing. This included collages and poems, stimulated by their gallery visit. Carole (high ability) read out her poem, to spontaneous applause, and various other presentations were made. Peter showed the researcher his poem about a waterfall. He explained that he had difficulty with writing and found it easier on the laptop. As lunchtime approached, Mr X brought the class together to talk about what they had done, and explain the afternoon's programme.

At *Rock High* Mrs Z, an English teacher, was with a Year 9 class of 20 pupils. They were in the middle of a six-week unit of work to develop a school guide for new (Year 7) pupils – work for a 'real audience'. She had a classroom assistant, Mrs Y, who happened to be a qualified primary teacher. Her main role was to support some lower ability pupils, but she also circulated to encourage extension work – the school had developed modules with core, extension and support materials in most subjects. After an initial discussion with the whole class, they got on with their tasks, Mrs Z and Mrs Y circulating to assist, offering help selectively. The pupils worked in pairs, planning their work and dividing up the tasks. These had been allocated with regard to pupil ability, so that everyone was expected to complete what they were asked to do. This approach, Mrs Z explained, was only feasible because the class had worked through a self-supported study unit the previous year.

In both these classrooms, pupils were encouraged and equipped to work with a degree of independence (from the teacher) and to collaborate, within a carefully planned framework. But there were many other classrooms, even in these schools which aimed to promote differentiation, where this was not the case, where all were set a common task with largely common materials, with little explanation of the learning goals. Alternatively, there were some primary classrooms where many pupils seemed confused by the variety of activities on offer in one session, with little evidence that this variety was meeting anyone's needs. How much responsibility can pupils be given in managing their learning? Can they be taught to be more effective learners – and to what extent do they currently understand what learning is about?

3.1 Teachers' Views of Pupil Competence: Survey Evidence

Primary heads and secondary heads of department in core subjects were asked to assess how many of their pupils (Year 6 and 8 respectively) were competent in various learning skills. They were also given the opportunity to say that the skills were not relevant in their context. This produced some interesting results. First, although almost all the primary heads and the heads of English in the secondaries saw all the skills as relevant, this was not the case with the secondary heads of science and maths. As Figure 3.1 shows, responses varied by subject and by skill. Less than three-quarters of the maths teachers saw it as relevant that Year 8 pupils should be agreeing learning targets or making presentations, and there was a similar reaction on target-setting and peer tutoring among science teachers. The most consistently relevant skills, for all groups, were seen as self-assessment, resource organisation and pair or group working.

Figure 3.1 Per cent of each subject group of teachers who thought the activity 'relevant' for Year 8 pupils

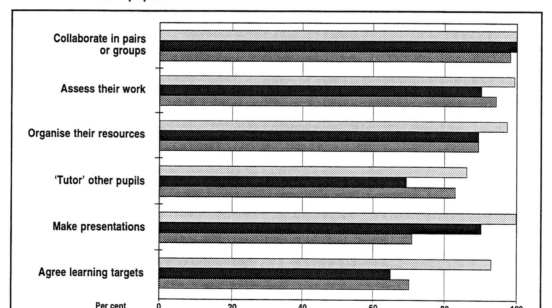

Based on responses from 559 heads of department.

46

Table 3.2 shows the percentage of each group who considered that 'most' pupils in the relevant year group were competent in each skill.

Table 3.2: Teachers' views of 'most' pupils' competence in managing their own learning

Pupils can competently	Primary HT Year 6 %	Sec. HOD Maths Year 8 %	Sec. HOD English Year 8 %	Sec. HOD Science Year 8 %
Collaborate in pairs or groups	72	58	76	83
Make presentations	50	10	64	27
Organise their own resources	48	36	28	29
Assess their work	33	35	38	21
Agree learning targets	18	13	34	10
'Tutor' other pupils	15	9	12	5
N =	405	175	163	187

A series of single response items.

There were significant differences between the secondary subject leaders for every skill. We shall refer to some of these in later parts of the chapter. Here we can note that heads of science were the most sceptical; although over 80 per cent thought that most pupils were competent at working in pairs or groups – a predictable aspect of science practice – less than one-third felt there was this level of competence for any of the other skills. Maths teachers were also fairly conservative about their pupils' skills (apart from pair-working). English teachers were more sanguine, and one-third thought that most pupils could agree learning targets – the only case where secondary staff were substantially more likely to see pupils as competent. In general, however, the results suggested that Year 6 pupils were more likely than the Year 8 pupils to be expected and found to be competent as independent learners. It is, of course, impossible to say whether these results tell us more about the actual behaviour of the pupils or about the expectations and perceptions of their teachers, but they certainly point to a significant difference in classroom cultures.

3.2   Diagnosing Needs and Reviewing Progress

According to most primary headteachers (85 per cent) and secondary heads of departments of maths (77 per cent), English (74 per cent) and science (64 per cent), assessment is wholly relevant to developing an effective strategy for differentiation (see also Chapter 4). Moreover, both primary and secondary schools apparently thought it appropriate for pupils to play a role in this process, through self-assessment. But whereas just over one-third of primary heads and heads of maths and English thought most such pupils can competently assess their work, only one-fifth of heads of science thought so. Why should this be so? Is it that certain subjects or teachers may utilise pupil review to a lesser degree? Or that the nature of some subjects makes this more difficult? If anything, one might expect more pupils to become competent in self-assessment as they get older; or is it that the skills of self-assessment may not be further developed in the secondary phase?

In their interviews, most of the 39 pupils interviewed could not talk easily about self-assessment. Primary pupils were usually involved in evaluating their own work to make up a folder of their achievements – 'at the end of term we have a brown envelope and we sort all the things out that we thought were good and that we would like to have as evidence of our work and things.' But they were mostly rather unsure about whether they were involved in self-appraisal or assessment. Despite this, pupils had a clear idea of where they ranked in the class group. A few students with learning difficulties who were closely monitored by learning support tutors did not see (or could not articulate) that they were involved in a target setting and review process, merely describing it as 'they just help you with the reading'. Pupils from *Hillside High* mentioned the Integrated Curriculum Assessment (ICA) scheme as helpful. This was a cross-curricular skills assessment system, in which pupils reviewed progress with their tutor once a term, across all subjects, using a common format (see Chapter 4). Some of them liked self-assessment as they felt it raised their awareness and self-esteem, helped to show what they were good at and what they were working towards as targets. In one primary school Year 6 pupils had Maths review sheets and concept maps which they reviewed at the end of term. In one secondary school, at the end of a module, Year 9 students assessed their English folders on effort, attainment and enjoyment.

> One mid-ability girl, reviewing her performance on a module on Romeo and Juliet, gave herself B for effort, 2 for attainment and A for enjoyment. She said she had completed most of the classwork to the best of her ability and that her best work was a

poster on display. She criticised her drawing. She set her targets for the following term as: presentation, to listen harder and to improve her spelling.

End of term reports were also mentioned by Year 4, 6 and 7 pupils as a way of knowing how they were progressing in their learning. In one primary school pupils were encouraged to write on their reports what they felt they had improved on and further suggestions for improvement.

Despite the efforts made in some schools to encourage pupils to review their own performance and progress, most of those interviewed reported that teacher comments, on their worksheets or in their books, or verbally directly to them, were the main source of knowing how they were getting on with their work. Secondary pupils were more likely to remark on the addition of grades or marks and that teacher comments were more frequent in some subjects (such as English and maths than personal and social education). A few pupils mentioned that they would have preferred face-to-face comments, rather than notes in their workbooks, but for others this made no difference. Many young people claimed that the advice they received from teachers' comments was 'helpful', 'encouraging', and gave targeted feedback, 'cos' I know what to aim for and improve on'. In some cases this led to a checklist of aspects which pupils could improve on. Some would have liked more feedback, especially in Maths, instead of 'just ticking it' or saying 'read the question again'. One bright Year 4 girl, aged 9, described a process of marking and continuous assessment and feedback which she shared with her class teacher, both at the end of a piece of work and when it was in progress:

> ... you usually go up to mark it. He will mark it while you are there so he will talk to you about how well you've done it and what else you need and the mistakes you've made.

> .. if I get stuck I go and tell him and he helps me work it out and when I'm marking it ... he'll give me a clue on what else I need to do and I have to work out how to do that.

Another fairly frequent way for pupils to know about their progress in learning is through results of tests. Weekly or fortnightly class tests for spelling, science and maths were mentioned by Year 4 or Year 6 pupils, and Year 9 students reported tests for English and Science at the end of modules of work. Two able Year 4 boys described their regular weekly spelling test:

> Sometimes he gives us about a 100 words spelling test ... He'll say spell 'then', watches and we write it down and if we're not sure about spelling a word we just have to guess it and then when he's over there ticking it and we're doing something else, he says

'Neil and Mark 100'. And if he says something like 98 a bit later he'll come and tell you what words you got wrong and he'll show you how to spell it.

Very few pupils remarked on teachers keeping records of their levels or grades, but the same Year 4 girl knew that:

He keeps a close eye on us to check whether we've achieved certain things in this book and he ticks them off as we go along.... yesterday we needed to learn about the growth of plants and we already did know that but we had to make sure everybody knew it to, you know, quite advanced.... to see what level you are at. And he doesn't mark the books with us but he tells us what we have to achieve sometimes in things like that...

Observant pupils quickly learned to pick up the signals from their teacher, and to assess whether they were on course. But what about the rest? The easiest indicators were numerical – marks in tests, numbered series of work cards. It was much harder for them to find the words to talk about skills they were developing or concepts they found hard to understand. Self-assessment as a procedure, where this was being developed, was not necessarily accompanied by teaching of the skills and the language to build an accurate profile of one's achievements and progress, and to refine this process over time. However, discussion in 'circle time' in primary schools and in some secondary lessons could help pupils to develop a proper critical appreciation of 'good work', their own and others'.

3.3 Knowing What to Do

In terms of knowing what they are attempting to achieve in a lesson or over a period of time, in the school survey, as we saw in Figure 3.1, around one-third of the heads of science and maths did not see the relevance of pupils' contribution to this area of the management of learning, even by the middle of Key Stage 3. But whereas 34 per cent of English teachers considered that most Year 8 pupils could agree learning targets competently, only 10 per cent of heads of science and 13 per cent of heads of maths agreed (Table 3.2). (Even if results are compared only for those heads of department who accepted the relevance of this goal, the proportion for maths and science is still less than 20 per cent.) The implication seems to be that in Key Stage 3 maths and science pupils do not usually have the opportunity to discuss learning targets or to show whether they can do this competently. It is perhaps not surprising that the younger pupils in Year 6 were mostly still developing this type of skill (only 20 per cent of heads thought most pupils were competent), but most primary heads saw agreeing learning targets as an appropriate goal for that age group.

The lack of involvement of pupils in setting learning targets, or even being clear what they were aiming at in lessons and how aspects of work fitted into a pattern, was evident from pupils' responses in interview. In some primary classes the timetable for the day was set out on a list on the board for the whole class or for groups of pupils. This approach was most fully developed in *Cottage Primary* – a two-teacher school with one class for each key stage – but a number of the primary case-study schools provided pupils individually with 'menus' of tasks. The head teacher believed in teaching all pupils, from five onwards, to manage their own materials and pursue tasks. This freed her to give more attention to each age group within the class for particular activities, such as maths work. But even though pupils knew what they were doing, it did not follow they understood why or what their specific learning target was. At secondary level, dependence on the teacher was even more marked. Most students acknowledged that teachers explained work at the beginning of the lesson. Interestingly, however, again the explanation covered what was to be done, not why. Some pupils would have found this an aid to their understanding and motivation. Similarly on most worksheets, which were ubiquitous, instructions tended to focus on procedures and content rather than the underlying goal or purpose of the task.

According to a Year 4 boy the teacher:

> ... gives us a rough idea of what you have to do. He doesn't tell us every single detail about it. He just tells us what you have to do, how to do it and then he says get on with it.

Having 'a rough idea' of what to do is not always enough for less able pupils. Another boy in the same class was reluctant to acknowledge that he did not always immediately grasp what to do, 'I could ask him to explain again when I don't quite understand it.' But he claimed he would ask 'when I really need to'. He needed encouragement and the repetition of what he was aiming for in a piece of work:

Y4B	Telling me twice and then I understand.
RES	What happens when you hear it the first time?
Y4B	I don't quite understand it.
RES	Is it because you feel nervous about what you've got to do?
Y4B	Yes.
RES	Do you think Mr [the teacher] understands that?
Y4B	I don't know because I haven't told him yet.

Elsewhere a Year 4 girl described what happened in her class:

Y4G After each break or after each subject thing our teacher says 'Come and sit on the carpet' and she'll tell us what to do next and she explains it all to us.

RES So she explains before you go away.

Y4G She says 'If you don't understand something put your hand up' and then you say what you don't understand and she'll explain it better to you.

At the secondary phase, especially, work sometimes continued into another lesson and teacher explanation was not always required:

...they explain what we've got to do in the lesson, but if we done it in the lesson before ..... then the next lesson they say 'Oh, just carry on with the work we were doing yesterday.' And in English at the moment because we're doing that Year 7 guide [for new pupils] we have to set our own homeworks, what we're going to do and do classwork . (Year 9, boy)

Many pupils were conscious that teachers tended to check up on their work as they went along, 'most of the time he walks around all of the class looking over their work'. However, this was not invariably the case. Pupils were aware of often being grouped by ability and the more able did not always see themselves as needing the teacher's attention whilst getting on with their work. The less able were more likely to acknowledge that they could ask for help from the teacher about what to do; the more able tended to ask about details. One mid-ability boy reflected on the importance of the teacher checking he was on course:

Y7B Some teachers think we can do it so they just leave it, they don't bother, but some teachers come and they help you out and say you're doing this wrong.

RES Which approach do you prefer do you think?

Y7B I like it when they come to you and tell you that, yes, ... because if you've done it and they go 'You've done it wrong', and you've got to do it all again and its not worth doing then.

RES Do you think it's important at times that you take responsibility for your own learning? Do you ever get the feeling that it's up to you to do things?

Y7B Yeah, sometimes. But it depends if you're doing it wrong, it's the teacher's duty to tell you that you're doing it wrong. So if you like don't understand it and you just do it wrong they've got to tell you that you're doing it wrong instead of waiting till you've finished. If you understand it's all right.

As was to be expected, older and more able pupils were more likely to find out for themselves what to do. They were more likely to see a pattern to their work and how they were building on their learning, which might be relevant to the real world or what they might need later in life.

3.4　Looking for Extra Help

Some young people needed additional support. Few pupils reported asking a friend to help with an explanation of what to do, but adults other than teachers were recognised for being able to give assistance. Even if Pupil or Learning Support Teachers were primarily in a class to help those who had learning needs, they were often seen as available to help all pupils if needed. Some saw this as meaning that they could get help quicker if the teacher was busy with someone else, and in some cases the teacher and the support teacher shared the class. One of the more able Year 9 boys recognised the usefulness of the Learning Support teachers 'cos it helps the other ones do better with their work'.

In *River High,* this was through a system of Pupil Support Teachers (PST). One Year 9 boy had been having help, especially with reading and spelling, in the Resource Centre and with in-class support for three years. He described how the teacher explained what to do in the lesson and 'if I'm not quite sure I ask her [the PST] as well, then the PST explained again 'she tries to help me like the teacher'. 'You need another teacher there with reading and writing, 'cos the teacher wouldn't be able to handle it.'

There were relatively few reports of parents working in school with pupils. One Year 4 boy who had difficulty with reading certain words and spelling had, with his mother's support, taken an initiative to help himself:

RES　　You had also written out some words yourself hadn't you on a card? ...How did you think about doing that? Did somebody suggest that to you?

Y4B　　No, its just that I wanted to remember words so I wrote them down on cards so I remembered them.

RES　　So you chose to write them on the card, ones you found.

Y4B　　Well my Mum thought of it as well.

Two parents of boys at *Observatory Primary* explained their reactions to their sons' involvement in the laptop project. One mother explained that it had given him a sense of responsibility, when he brought the laptop home, not allowing his siblings to play with it. Her son, she felt, was 'normally keen and disheartened if he can't do something. If he can do something, he wants more of it and harder.' By contrast, the other boy's mother was well aware of her son's learning difficulties which showed up in poor spelling. Unbeknown to the school, she had been helping her son, who had also been receiving an hour's paid tuition a week. She felt the laptop was little help to him at home, and was torn between her desire to get him the help he needed and 'making a fuss'.

While the schools – especially primary schools – were keen to involve parents in their children's learning and took care to explain changes and special provision to them, few seemed to have regular opportunities for individual review, outside the customary parents' evening. One exception was *Rock High* which introduced 'profiling sessions' for parents and pupils with the group tutor. However, at the time of the study these sessions did not focus directly on classroom learning.

3.5 Choice and Time Management

If pupils are going to pursue different tasks within one classroom, or work in different ways in carrying out a task, either there has to be a very high degree of teacher management or the pupils themselves have to have been taught to organise themselves to work in this way, with some degree of control over their resources and the use of time. We wanted to know if teachers saw pupils as competent in this respect, and also how pupils themselves felt about the degree of choice they had in how they worked. Whether or not a degree of pupil autonomy is relevant to differentiation depends on whether teachers recognise its value as a tool for increasing the effectiveness of the individual learner, and expanding the opportunities for purposeful differential approaches in the classroom as a whole.

Around 40 per cent of primary heads and secondary heads of departments considered pupils' organisational skills are 'wholly relevant' to developing an effective strategy for differentiation, although, once again, there were some subject differences, with more heads of English (45 per cent) than Maths (34 per cent) making this judgement. When asked about pupils' competence in organising their own resources (see Table 3.2), primary heads again seemed to have a higher opinion than secondary heads of department of pupils' organisational skills; about half of the former considered that most Year 6 pupils could competently organise their resources. Year 8 pupils were less likely to be seen as competent. For maths, just over a third (36 per cent) of the heads of department saw most of their pupils as competent, and in English and science it was less than 30 per cent.

Some of the difference between primary and secondary perspectives may well relate to the contrast in classroom and curriculum management, with more apparent opportunities and indeed requirements in many primary classrooms for pupils to manage resources and make choices. When asked if they could choose different ways to work in a lesson, when this might happen and why, about a quarter of those pupils interviewed did not see themselves as having any choice about how to work. Some saw themselves as sometimes having some choices. This may have been a matter on which some pupils, especially those who were younger or less able, were not accustomed to reflect or comment, but it could also relate to a teaching and learning culture in which young people see themselves as doing 'what the teacher tells us to do'. A few interviewees were conscious that learning tasks or processes could be different according to ability (sets, pupil with special needs with helper), subject, groupings within class and materials (e.g. in maths getting an answer by using cubes, fingers and toes, calculators or working it out in one's head). Investigations in science, history and English were seen as offering choices. English was most often mentioned as an arena for choice.

Choices specifically mentioned by pupils included:

♦   choice of task (also asking to do something different);

♦   choice of order of task (e.g. three in a certain time in any order);

♦   choice within task of what to do and how to do it (e.g. writing or drawing, story or poem) choice of who to work with;

♦   choice of resource (e.g. of worksheet);

♦   choice of how to present work (e.g. written (in rough, in best), typed on computer, orally);

♦   choice of which work to finish;

♦   choice of what to do after finishing work set (e.g. doing work or playing games on computer);

♦   choice of which work to revise.

In their review of pupil experience in Key Stage 1 classrooms, Pollard *et al.* (1994) discussed this issue of choice, and found that Year 2 pupils were more likely than the younger ones to feel their choice was restricted (the teacher chooses). Again, there were a number of unresolved issues about the purposes choice was serving, even at this early age; for example, whether it should be a reward for finishing 'work'. In our study, some students were aware of when they might not be allowed to choose how to work. For example, one Year 4 less able boy knew that they could not always work with partners or in small groups, 'Well, sometimes we know when he says "No" it's maybe because the work is in the blue folder that we have [National Curriculum SATs] and it says work on your own.' Choice could be a motivation for learning. One Year 9 boy liked to choose the order of his work 'because you find it more interesting. You do like something first and then like you're into it and then you get into the deeper part of it.' Others related choice to doing what they are good at or future goals. Another Year 9 boy of higher ability claimed that pupils nearly always had a choice of what to do 'not all the time, it depends what subject. When we're doing projects, History, we can do it in a binder, in a collage like we have all different writing and things, booklet, like a newspaper. I usually do that 'cos I'm thinking about being a journalist when I leave school.'

Even where the pupils had an extra dimension of choice, in the classroom equipped with laptops, familiar patterns could readily emerge. Thus in follow-up work based on *The Secret Garden*, it was the pupils who had finished their other work on the book who could choose to use the art software on the computers to design their own garden.

Pace of work and time management can be an issue for some pupils. Many of those interviewed claimed that they sometimes finished their work early. Whether they did or not seemed to depend on the combination of several factors, such as ability, the subject, the particular task, and the time allowed. If they finished early some pupils reported that they would ask the teacher what to do; they might be told to check their work or use the time to catch up. A few reported that they would have a choice of what to do if they finished early and some favoured using computers, perhaps to redraft their work. One bright Year 4 girl reported:

RES   So if you finish early are there other things that you go on to do?

Y4G   Yeah, sometimes if you do something quickly, that is a main thing, and if there aren't any things you can do involved with it, then if it's quite near the end you can read or something, but sometimes you can choose what you want to do.

RES   So say if you finished your Maths problem early, you could go and read if you wanted, you wouldn't necessarily have to do Maths?

Y4G   Or you could do handwriting. That's what I usually do if I've got a little bit of spare time left. If I've got more time than that I would finish some work rather than doing a little thing because it's a waste of good time if you've finished your work.

Several pupils across the age range indicated that they would be told to read if they finished their work early. In one school this might mean going to the Listening Centre. In some schools and in certain subjects (perhaps particularly maths, but English, French, history and religious education were also mentioned) if pupils finished early they were given, or could choose, extension work. In French a boy finished a dialogue and was given a crossword to do. In English a Year 9 mid-ability girl reported that in one instance when she had finished early the teacher gave her extension work related to the topic, a spidergram about the novel 'Wolf', her own spidergram, and answering the question 'What does the cover of the book tell you about the story?' Alternatively, she might choose extension work from a pack on the classroom wall. According to a bright Year 9 boy this work was at different levels: 'In Maths there'd be different levels, like 4,5,6,7 – depends, higher level harder it gets – but in English I think they're all the same, which might be write a story, or they give you poems or something.' He claimed extension work was motivating 'cos we get to learn more' and it was related to merit marks, which in turn could be exchanged for items at the school shop!

These comments on choice and the pay-off for 'finishing early' illustrate the complex motivations at work. If the pay-off is seen to be limited or boring (more of the same), then stringing the work out to fill the time available can seem the best strategy. But even young children apparently learn the advantages of getting the 'teacher's work' over quickly so they can do something easier or more appealing (Pollard et al., 1994). On the other hand, planned extension work clearly could be intrinsically motivating. Another option – that work was designed to be interesting and challenging throughout, so that 'extension' did not mean 'extra' – was difficult to pursue in interview. As we shall see in the next chapter, it was a concept that was central to the differentiation strategy in several schools.

Many pupils also acknowledged that they did not always finish their work in the time available. For instance, one less able Year 4 boy who found it difficult 'sometimes when I can't figure out what to do, not to do, but I can't describe it in the work.' For some there was a long-term and ongoing sense of frustration; one less able Year 9 reported, 'Sometimes when I haven't finished my work I get a bit angry because I'm such a slow writer. Other people I know they write really fast so they get ahead.' A few pupils said they would ask the teacher for help but sometimes the teacher was not the first port of call: 'I would maybe talk about it with my friend, or the person I am sitting next to, or the person opposite me. If I was really stuck then I would go and ask a teacher.' If work was not finished some pupils reported they stayed in at break or lunch time to complete it, add to it, or embellish it. Sometimes, particularly at the secondary phase pupils were allowed extra time to continue the work in another lesson or they were told to finish it at home or in a free period. A few, however noted that sometimes work was left unfinished. On the whole they preferred to finish their work and copy it out neatly and some saw that they might miss out on a mark if they did not finish the work.

Homework was clearly seen by some pupils as a way of compensating for insufficient time in class. Although some pupils had homework in Year 4, this was an activity more associated with the secondary phase and it could involve finishing off work after a lesson or at the end of the week – for those unlucky enough to have work outstanding. But there were other issues relevant for pupils about working at home. They were somewhat divided, apparently by ability, about whether they preferred working at home or at school. The more able tended to prefer working at home: 'you can go at your own pace', or 'because they don't disturb you at home ... and I can concentrate more at home'. The motivation of some depended on what was to be done. One or two even welcomed something to be done at home. One Year 7 boy in a lower band had proved to be surprisingly able in maths. He had taken to asking the teacher for extra problems and investigations he could work on at home. In *Observatory Primary,* where Year 4 were involved with a project using laptops, pupils took it in turns to take the laptops home. This was highly motivating to pupils of all abilities and, as we have seen, could surprise their parents. One mid-ability boy had written several stories, done Maths on spreadsheets and explored 'goodies', such as chess and patience. Others found it harder to work on their own at home and felt less confident about their abilities or could not get help. These pupils were more likely to prefer working at school 'because a teacher is there to help' if they got stuck. This applied all the more so if they had pupil support, and such pupils were likely to do all or part of their homework in the resource centre. Some pupils also preferred doing certain subjects in school. For example, one Year 7 girl of mid-ability said, 'In science I rather like doing it at school 'cos like when the teacher explains to you can understand it more.'

3.6   Changing Roles

One way of enabling all pupils to engage fully in learning and to demonstrate a range of capabilities is to vary the roles which they are asked to take. A large majority of primary heads and heads of department of core subjects (70-80 per cent) claimed that with Key Stage 2 and Key Stage 3 pupils they only sometimes or occasionally found varying pupil roles (such as presenting, tutoring, evaluating) practicable strategies for meeting pupils' individual learning needs. Again there was considerable variation between subjects, and about 20 per cent of heads of maths claimed that such strategies were not used in their departments. Chapter 4 discusses possible reasons for these patterns from the teachers' perspective.

The issue of pupil competence is particularly relevant here. Pupils were hardly likely to demonstrate or improve their competence in a variety of roles if they did not get the opportunity. But why were opportunities apparently restricted? Was it because of unavoidable constraints of time, space and pressure to cover the curriculum? Or did teachers see some roles as irrelevant to effective learning? The survey responses in Figure 3.1 and Table 3.2 indicate possible explanations.

One possibility was difference of approach between subjects. We have seen that secondary maths leaders were less likely to provide opportunities for role-changing. This was corroborated by evaluations of the extent to which teachers saw pupils as able to contribute to the management of their own learning by *making presentations.* The response of heads of maths differed markedly from other subjects as over one-quarter did not even see this as relevant for Year 8 pupils and only one in ten thought that most pupils could competently make presentations. By contrast, half the primary heads and the majority of heads of English (64 per cent) considered most pupils could do this (only a quarter – 27 per cent – of heads of science thought so).

Changing the pupil role often involved *pupils working together.* Here the evidence was conflicting. An overwhelming majority of primary heads and secondary heads of core subject departments expected pupils to work in pairs or groups and – except in maths – generally felt that most pupils could do this. Observational experience suggests that in maths lessons pupils are more likely to work individually, reinforcing the pattern of subject differences. But it is now widely accepted that sitting together is not the same as working collaboratively. In the great majority of lessons we observed, pupils were grouped round tables, as if they were intended to collaborate. But for the great majority of time, they were working individually (if socially) rather than sharing a task. We asked pupils how much opportunity they had to work with others. We also asked teachers about pupils' skills in collaborating.

One particular type of paired work involves *peer tutoring*. For the teacher respondents in the survey this was the least prevalent role for pupils, although (with the exception of science) over 80 per cent considered that at least some pupils could act as competent 'tutors'. Very few considered most Year 6/8 pupils could do so, particularly in secondary school (see Figure 3.2).

Figure 3.2: Teachers' views of Year 6 and Year 8 pupils' competence as peer tutors

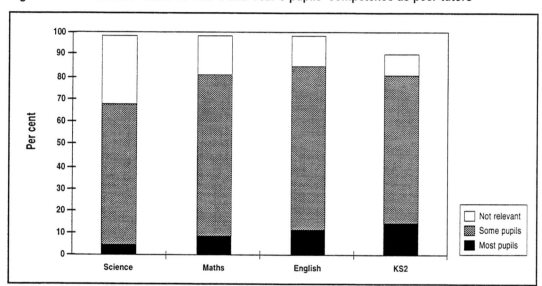

Pupils reported that they experienced learning situations on their own, in pairs and in small groups. Young people as a whole were divided about whether they learnt more on their own or working with others. Some preferred working individually because they liked to have the ideas, knew that they got it right and were anxious that in a pair they might get it wrong, or didn't like having to share or work with others' ideas. Whilst there was a tendency for the more able to feel this way, the less able could get a strong sense of satisfaction from having their own ideas. One Year 4 boy said he worked best, 'Sometimes when I'm on my own, because the other partner might have a different idea, but when you are on your own you can just have that one idea.'   Others did not like getting their work copied, and liked to get the credit for their work – 'So people don't copy you and they get commendation points and you don't get them.' Some felt that they did not concentrate so well in groups and were concerned that 'people can boss you around in groups'. One Year 4 boy of mid-ability thought 'I probably work best on my own. Because sometimes you mess around and don't concentrate. And they make you laugh.' These comments seem to point to the conflict which can arise from inappropriate seating: that is, being expected to complete the same individual, non-collaborative (no copying) task in a social seating arrangement.

Working in pairs was fairly common for the whole or part of a common task. The extent of this practice varied by subject, with English being the most recognised forum. Pairs could be of equal ability, or one might act as a peer tutor to the other. Thus for some it was a matter of 'finding things out together' which was helpful, easier and led to 'getting the job done quicker'.

> Sometimes in maths it is useful having a partner as someone else might know.

> M and I usually work together. He shows me if I've done a bit wrong.

> I don't mind on my own, but if I'm in a two I like it 'cos we discuss ideas.

> If you're working on your own you can concentrate a bit more, but it depends like if you're allowed to talk or what. But if you're working in pairs then if you don't know something someone else might know the answer.

In peer tutoring it was a question of the more able helping the less able. Sometimes this was on a task from the beginning, but sometimes pupils were asked to help another pupil when they had already finished, or were still doing their own work. The latter could cause some disquiet. There were advantages for the less able who were able to finish their work early. One Year 4 boy said, 'I like about it that we can share work and it can be a lot neater because if one of them is better at writing than drawing it can happen like that.' The more able could also learn things by helping the less able and come to have a better appreciation of their qualities and skills. Two able Year 4 boys who were discovering their abilities on the computer spoke about an episode when they worked with another boy to make a 3D noughts and crosses board.

> Y4B1   It was nice to work with another person.

> Y4B2   Because we're always working together, so it was a bit of a change to work with someone else as well.

> RES   What did you learn about working with him?

> Y4B2   We learnt a lot about D... We learn how quick he can do things.

> Y4B1   We learn how quick he is at work. We learn his disabilities and his abilities at work and we also find out what he can do right, what he can do wrong. What he needs help on, what he doesn't ...I said to him, 'D I want you to something, you've got a target. I want you to find some material and build eight legs.'...He said 'Straws' and then he said 'Oh, no, I can't get them because we haven't got any.'

Y4B2	And then D went straight over to Mr P and asked 'Do you have any straws?', didn't he?
Y4B1	And Mr P said 'No'. So he got some paper and rolled it up. It was all measured out and he rolled it up and he glued the bottom and he stuck it onto the board. And then we had one board, with two there and two there. We glued the tops, and stuck another one, and put four again, and stuck another one on.
Y4B2	Until it came a 3D board.
RES	So what did you learn about his idea of how to do it?
Y4B2	Well we know that D is very good at modelling. We just left him to build the eight legs while we were just fitting the boards and getting the glue and stuff.

Some said they preferred working in pairs to being in a small group. Pupils were divided about whether their friends should partner them. Some considered it was difficult because they tended to argue. As one Year 4 girl put it:

> Well sometimes – this sounds quite funny – with a friend you argue more about what you're going to do and things. If you are with someone who you are not really friends with you just get along with them. If you didn't get along with them that wouldn't be very good, but if you can work with them I find that better because you don't know each other so well and you're not arguing so much.

Others liked discussing ideas with their friends. One mid-ability Year 9 girl liked working with her friend, Lisa, who worked at a similar pace and rate although she reckoned she was 'a bit cleverer because she's in higher sets in Maths and geography.' 'If I work on my own sometimes I get a bit confused and that and I ask Lisa and she helps me and if she's working faster than me it makes me catch up more.'

Working in small groups was a common experience for some pupils, but only occasional for others. It was mentioned as occurring in design and technology, science, English, music, maths, art and RE. Mostly small group work took place for discussions in English, project or topic work and investigations in maths – an exception, perhaps, to the predominant pattern of individual 'seatwork'. Some pupils thought it made work 'easier and you get it down quicker' or 'you can tell if you could do better'. Team work was not common, although some reported working in groups of seven in drama.

One bright Year 4 girl summarised the pros and cons of individual, paired and small group learning:

Y4G   ...if we are working in a big group we help each other sometimes or talk about it with each other and ... we always have to do one of each thing for each person usually if we work in pairs. But we always help each other usually and... so you learn it's not copying ... if you've found something out you share it with everyone else and you learn how to do that....

RES   What do you think is useful about that way of working?

Y4G   ...I like practical learning because ... it's usually work that you're making things .. or you can talk about it with a friend and you understand it a lot better because it's not just someone telling you things, it's you finding out for yourself and that's good because I learn a lot more that way.

Some teachers, particularly in primary school, were keen to promote group work, encouraging pupils to act as group leaders in carrying out tasks. But for the pupils this seemed to be at best an occasional experience, and the paired working often seemed to be an informal arrangement, rather than a strategy planned by the teacher.

Using resources

In an attempt to consider the learning approaches and resources which individuals found effective, we asked the pupils 'What things help you most to learn?' A range of resources, which pupils could experience passively or interactively were mentioned. These included: worksheets, textbooks, the library or resource centre, books, video, audio tapes and recorders, computers, calculators. Calculators were mentioned fairly often by Year 3 to 6, computers by Year 4 and 6, videos and books by Year 6 and 9.

Worksheets, which were ubiquitous, were sometimes valued because they gave 'more detail' or acted as revision sheets for the less able. Textbooks were useful 'because they explain what to do', but were no substitute for a communicative teacher. Although books were seen as helpful by many, the less able found that they were 'too much reading'. By the secondary years, most claimed that they knew their way around the resource centre or library and were self-reliant. 'It'll help you work when you're older if you learn to take responsibility at this stage.' One or two made use of dictionaries or encyclopaedias, though the CD-ROM Encarta was beginning to supplant the latter in young people's affections.

On the whole, there was little reported experience of use of audio cassettes and tape recorders, although they were used in English, for example, in constructing radio plays. By contrast, the viewing of videos, especially in English and the humanities, was widespread and was claimed to be helpful for supplying information. Although viewing could be a passive experience, pupils reported note taking, sometimes as a prelude to acquiring other more specific information, or as a reminder. Whilst some placed videos on a par with reading, others said they were 'better than a book – it shows it to you' and that the video was 'easier to remember'.

Computers were used, often with enthusiasm and skill, in a range of ways – for writing, redrafting, copying work, reading, spelling, in maths, or for playing games and having fun. In some schools their use was restricted by availability or technical problems. Sometimes using the computer was kept as a reward. Where their use was integrated into teaching they seemed to be perceived by pupils of all abilities as helpful, whether it was because they supported the less able in writing and spelling, mid-ability pupils to do work at their own level and pace, or the high fliers to do sophisticated tasks more simply or quickly.

One Year 9 pupil who had had learning support throughout the secondary school, claimed that he liked computers because 'you can get information. I find it a lot easier than looking things up in books.' In science he had seen some information on the computer 'so I decided to do about the stomach, so I got a picture scanned and I found out all the different parts of the stomach and the tract.' Others who needed support found the spell checker 'fun and it helps you to spell better'. It seemed to help with incremental learning 'It's helpful. It gives you the word you've spelt wrong and it gives you lists.' However, an able Year 4 girl who liked to use the computer 'for stories and things because you've got a wide range of different styles of writing in size and layout and its easier because I can type with two fingers' was able to appraise the advantages and disadvantages of using the spell checker:

> You've got a spellchecker but sometimes that doesn't help with your spelling because you know you can always check it, you don't try so hard sometimes to get the spelling right. I always try to get the spelling right or I always have a go at getting the spelling right ... its useful to have a spellcheck if you do that. But if you have the wrong attitude to it and you think 'It doesn't matter if I write every word in this wrong I can always spell check it.' But you still have to be careful about punctuation and things because you don't have a check for that, you can only check for spellings, so you have to be careful in what way you are laying out and all the other things apart from spelling.

Some Year 4 pupils had started to see the computer as a tool to aid and support their learning, an alternative to other sources:

> What's good about it is if you are not sure about a word and you're going to write it down. If it's a really long word it's better to go on the computer, write down the word in the word processor and spell check it instead of getting out a dictionary looking at all these really long words. And if you want to do something like the 5000 times table if the number gets too big for the calculator you go on the spreadsheet, write it down times five, you just make the square really big and the answer will come really massive.

Other Year 4 pupils, like this boy, had become quite sophisticated in using the computer at school and at home as a learning aid and could explain how they had discovered certain complex mathematical functions. Others relied on calculators and other forms of counting equipment. Some said that they learned from games in maths.

One Year 4 girl, speaking in relation to learning to work with the computer recognised that this had generated a learning community where the pupils and teachers were working together as co-learners:

> One time I had to help somebody with something quite difficult and Mr X came along too and we worked the problem out together and that helps me learn as well I think.

Pupils proved perceptive critics of the resources on offer to them, and in particular were apparently becoming aware quite quickly of the value of computers as tools for information retrieval as well as a range of other purposes. On the other hand, they seemed to accept the more mundane materials on which they spent most of their time as an inevitable part of school life. From these conversations, there were indications that many of them would be able to handle more challenging resources, once they had been taught how to use them. On the other hand, the fear of books with 'too much reading' was very real for some pupils.

3.7   Reviewing the Pupils' Perspective

We have deliberately started our main evidence with the pupils' perspective, to stress the potential importance of their contribution to the underlying purpose of raising attainment. That is, not just their effort and application, but what they bring to the learning process. These conversations and observations of pupils at work suggest that, just as pupils have proved perceptive about 'what makes a good teacher' (Taylor, 1996) so they have useful comments to make about what helps them to learn. What came through, from their own comments and from teachers' views in the survey on the skills which they thought most pupils could demonstrate, was how relatively dependent pupils were on the teacher, both for organising their work and for help in carrying it out. And yet, there were plenty of indications that pupils could and did organise themselves effectively, supported each other in their work and made suggestions about how to carry it forward – all these being more likely to occur, on the whole, in Key Stage 2 than in Key Stage 3 classrooms. Moreover, there seemed to be far less stigma than might be imagined, at least among the primary pupils, in asking learning support staff for help.

Perhaps the most striking contrast, in the pupil comments in this chapter, is between the pupils who were articulate and observant (not always the high ability pupils) and proved 'streetwise' (or 'classwise'), and those who apparently needed to be taught the relevant skills of managing their own learning and the art of working productively with others. What seemed to be missing was just that kind of instruction and indeed a climate in which it was natural to make learning targets explicit and to spell out the criteria for success. They appreciated the feedback of one-to-one review from the teacher, perhaps particularly because, in the absence of such criteria, this was the only source of judgement. They were mostly unsure about self-assessment, working out their place in the class 'pecking order' from external indicators – work undertaken, marks given. They seemed to be more like a group of holiday makers on a package tour, dependent on their guide for information and planning, than a company of backpackers with maps and railway timetables.

4. PLANNING AND RESPONDING: THE TEACHERS' TASK

4.1 Principles, Planning and Practice

The purpose of this chapter is to review the ways in which teachers plan and implement strategies which foster differentiation. We were continually faced with the problem of holding together principles and classroom practice. What did teachers feel their aims were, in principle? Could these aims be realised in practice? More specifically, to what extent did teachers plan differentiation into their work beforehand (and how did they do this?); or was differentiation mainly a matter of responding to pupils differentially, once the lesson was underway?

The chapter draws on case-study evidence (lesson observations, evidence gained from interviews with teachers, attendance at meetings) and the survey responses. As Chapter 2 explained, a core list of classroom differentiation strategies or mechanisms was devised during the exploratory stage of the project, and used in classroom observation, interviews and survey. In addition, teachers' perceptions about their practice and the factors which might influence it were explored. During the interviews, for example, teachers were asked to comment on the context and resources which might influence what they did to implement differentiation in the classroom, such as curriculum planning, pupil grouping, classroom management and the use of diagnostic assessment and resources. Some of these issues were followed up in the survey. However, while the interviews included teaching staff with a range of experience and seniority (as well as some teaching assistants), the survey was targeted at senior managers and (in secondary schools) middle managers (heads of department).

We wanted to review what teachers intend to do in order to implement their differentiation principles, before they engage with their classes, and then what they actually do in the classroom. We were therefore interested in the *planned* strategies teachers employ to meet the range of learning needs, such as the preparation of a range of curriculum materials, deciding upon and arranging for peer tutoring or pre-arranged groupings within the class, and the *responsive* aspects of teaching. These are not necessarily explicitly planned by teachers, although they are an integral part of the classroom strategies they normally use. It is quite usual for teacher to have built into their planning the fact that some of these flexible responses will be used, although the detail of preparation is different from that undertaken for the *planned* strategies.

It is worth recalling at this stage how teachers felt about the principle of differentiation, as discussed in Chapter 2. Through the survey, we have their views indirectly. Although the primary questionnaire was completed by the headteacher or senior managers, they were asked to consult their Key Stage 2 teachers about these responses. Similarly, the secondary heads of department of English, maths and science were asked to discuss these principles with their subject colleagues. Given the marked differences between the responses of the secondary subject staff and the secondary heads or senior managers, there is some ground for thinking that they did so.

The two principles which staff felt best expressed what differentiation was *mainly* about, it may be remembered, were 'raising the attainment of all pupils' and 'planning learning to match individuals' needs'. There was also another principle, more directly linked to teaching methods: that differentiation was mainly about improving teaching methods to suit the task. Obviously, these shorthand definitions are difficult to respond to, but this provided an opportunity to focus clearly on pedagogy (the most effective methods and resources for all *these* learners, for *this* task) as the starting point for planned differentiation. As Figure 4.1 shows, most staff agreed that this was important, but the secondary teaching staff were much less likely than the senior managers to put a strong emphasis on improving teaching methods to suit the task. As in other questions, the English specialists were the nearest to their primary colleagues in their views.

Figure 4.1: **Is differentiation *mainly* about improving teaching methods to suit the task? Views of various staff groups**

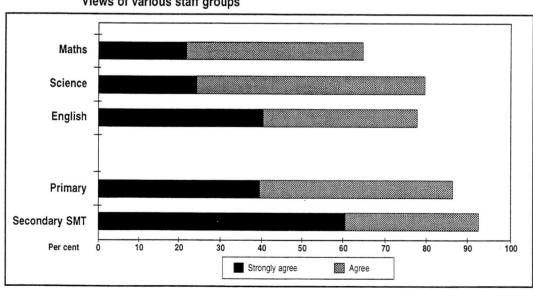

Based on responses by heads of core subjects (secondary) and their Key Stage 3 teachers, primary heads and their Key Stage 2 teachers and secondary senior managers.

4.2 Planning for Differentiation

In this section we consider how teachers' principles were applied in curriculum planning, mainly by departments and teams. The most obvious starting point was the principle that it was mainly 'about planning learning to match individual pupils' needs'. Not only did this interpretation show how committed most teachers were to the aim of meeting *individual* needs, it also drew attention to the *planning* of learning. This was especially important when considering how teachers planned *for differentiation*, within the general framework of planning for teaching.

An important issue here was the management of curriculum planning for each class and subject. Who took part? How much say did most classroom teachers have over content and approach? In other words, to what extent could they plan for differentiation? In some schools, decisions had been taken at senior management level which shaped the context for their planning; in particular, decisions about ability grouping (see Chapter 5). But whatever the context, it was the responsibility of middle managers, usually subject specialists and co-ordinators, to organise the planning of schemes of work. We found that curriculum planning was generally systematic and formalised throughout the case-study schools. This was certainly the case at the strategic level – designing modules/topics units to satisfy National Curriculum and school-defined requirements; there was more variety in what classroom teachers did at the tactical level – shaping lessons to adapt schemes of work to particular classes.

Strategic planning occurred either at departmental, curriculum co-ordinator or at year-group level, depending on the subject and school phase. Planning focused mainly on content, with teachers coming together to decide what topics they needed to cover and what were the best activities and resources to use in order to achieve the coverage. There were different approaches in primary or secondary schools mainly because of the organisational needs of various institutions.

Planning for differentiation in secondary schools

In secondary schools, approaches to detailed curriculum planning varied considerably between subjects, as well as between schools. In some cases, strategic planning had been 'top-down': undertaken by one teacher – often the head of department – on behalf of the rest. This provided others, particularly new teachers or part-timers, with a solid bank of materials and a framework for their teaching. On the other hand, some teachers found it hard to implement such a highly specified schema, especially when they had had no part in developing it. In interviews, they implied that there was little scope for planning – it was more a question of meeting requirements. Much depended on the time designated for departmental review and development, and how this was used by subject teams.

Figure 4.2   Key Stage 3 lesson planning in three secondary subjects

English

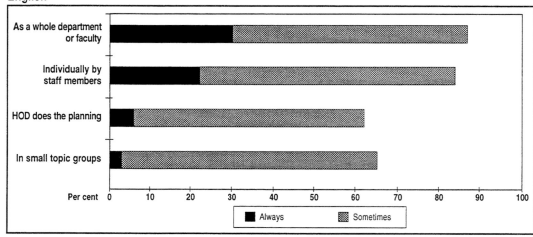

Maths

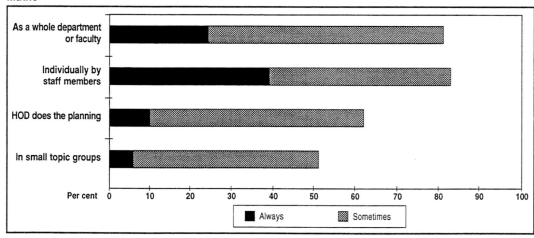

Science

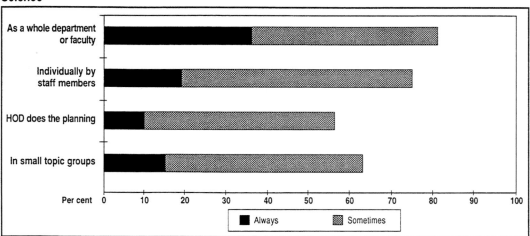

For this reason, we asked heads of departments in the survey about the pattern of Key Stage 3 lesson planning in their departments and who took part. They were asked about four possible patterns, and whether these were 'always', 'sometimes' or 'never' used. The percentage who 'always' or 'sometimes' used each one are shown in Figure 4.2.

The responses suggest that there was no dominant pattern that was 'always' used in any of the three subjects. Not surprisingly, different approaches would probably be used, for example, for longer-term planning and work on lessons for each teacher's classroom. But some patterns are evident. Across the three core subjects, less than 40 per cent of respondents said that the whole department or faculty were 'always' involved in planning, but for English and science this was the preferred approach along with individual planning, pointing to the complementary approach for overall planning and detailed application. Another variant was for the head of department to take on the overall planning, which happened 'sometimes' in about half the schools. Maths teachers seemed to have the greatest autonomy in the area of lesson planning, with 39 per cent of their heads of department reporting that lesson planning was 'always' done individually. From the observations in the case-study schools this may be because many mathematics departments followed a published course or had adapted published materials for their own closely specified programme. This ensured that heads of department were aware that individual lessons had to fit within this framework. Further planning was therefore tactical and heads of department expected it to be carried out by individual class teachers, as they got to know their pupils and interpreted the plan accordingly Conversely, science and English teams were more likely 'always' to plan together, as a faculty.

Perhaps the issue, in relation to differentiation, is one of ownership. Whether the department has devised its own scheme of work or works mainly from a published programme or course, the challenge is to enable each teacher to make it their own and find the scope to adapt it for the pupils they know and teach.

The need to take account of (strategic) departmental planning of schemes of work with differentiation in mind and (tactical) classroom planning by the teacher to meet the needs of a particular class had been clearly identified at *Rock High,* where the differentiation working party had agreed that differentiation 'needed to be carefully planned into each unit of work' (for more details of the school's overall strategy, see also Chapter 6). In other words, teachers needed to start from a scheme of work which made the range of requirements explicit and provided resources or tools for meeting them.

◆ At departmental level, approaches which had been successful included deciding on core elements of units, providing a range of resources or creating a differentiated range of tasks. At classroom level a long list was provided of possible ways of planning for differentiation within the departmental framework. These included variations in pace, in use of in-class groupings, use of peer support and IT, as well as use of in-class support.

The variation in approach between subjects was very evident at this and another school which both made differentiation a high priority but accepted different classroom contexts for planning.

At *Hillside High,* approaches to planning were always framed by the need to consider the four ability bands into which most Key Stage 3 pupils were grouped, as well as National Curriculum requirements. At a school level, there was a move during the year of the study to 'unitise' the curriculum, that is, to develop modules with targets appropriate to varying levels of ability, and each department responded in its own way. The mathematics department had remodelled its scheme of work into modules. The head of department had found the School Mathematics Project (SMP) scheme dull and relentless as the sole provision, and the new system was designed to offer a more flexible and varied approach. The framework was the same for all classes and – in topics – for Year 7 and 8. Each unit was designed to last for three weeks and had the same format:

◆ Introductory lead lesson with diagnostic test (*'Can you...?'*);

◆ Individual working, with start-point and route determined by outcome of test (1-2 weeks) with mini-test on completion of each booklet. Staff had created a box of resources and graded booklets for each topic;

◆ Summary lesson, with common notes on unit for whole class;

◆ Final test, with a choice of three test levels.

He felt this structure provided a balance of individual and class work as well as catering for all levels of attainment. In principle, the banding system was irrelevant, since all pupils were working through the same topics and drawing on the same resources, which covered all ability levels. This detailed planning of the overall framework and the resources meant that staff in the department had relatively little scope or need for further planning for their class. On the other hand, they might feel constrained by the 'lockstep' structure of three-week units, needing to move on the next unit regardless of pupils' progress. Since the same topic would be 'revisited' in Year 8, the head of department thought this was acceptable.

The science department at this school had also opted for units of work which aimed to link the ability grouping with National Curriculum levels. Here again the head of department had taken the lead in creating a scheme of work for Key Stage 3, in which each science teacher covered all three subject areas (biology, chemistry, physics) in order to maintain continuity of teaching for the class. The units were common for all the ability bands, but targets had been set, before the Dearing Review (1994), at Level 4-7, with a broad target level for each of the four bands; in all, 24 of the 41 modules had been differentiated to some extent. Lesson objectives and methods were made explicit for teachers, who were encouraged to review them at informal weekly meetings. The greatest obstacle to the development of planned differentiation, in this head of department's view, was the lack of time to work together as a department. By the end of the 1994-95 year, these units were being re-written to meet post-Dearing requirements and the concept of core plus extension and support introduced for every unit.

These two schemes were essentially top-down approaches, mainly initiated by heads of department. In the English department of the same school, one of the main grade English teachers had been given the responsibility and temporary financial enhancement to develop differentiated units of work. However, within a broad curriculum framework which stipulated some differences in input for each band (in terms of the literature they were to study), each of the 10 teachers had some latitude in planning work for his or her class. They could draw on a range of resource materials which were increasingly being identified by National Curriculum level. To monitor and evaluate progress, one lesson a week was devoted to departmental review.

At *Rock High*, where departments could decide themselves how pupils should be grouped (justifying their approach to the senior management team by showing how it met a common set of criteria, see Chapter 6), there were again marked differences of approach between subjects.

The English department, which had five years earlier introduced a modularised scheme of work and was working with mixed ability groups throughout the school, chose to differentiate materials and teaching at three levels – the main path, the supported path and the extension path. The head of department emphasised that the extension work was not just for the more able; the class folder had a range of extension work at various levels. Moreover, the department had arranged occasional Saturday extension sessions on a voluntary basis, for pupils of all abilities. Planning at departmental level was extensive, and included leaflets for pupils setting out the tasks to be completed for each. A class teacher explained how she adapted the module for her class, working with the support teacher to whom she gave a lesson plan for half a term's work. She thought it was easier to differentiate if there was a common programme, and stressed the importance of having a range of resources. She already had a particular departmental responsibility for text books and, with a colleague, was going to have one period a week during 1995-96 to spend on developing support materials. The head of department said that the 10 staff in the department regarded planning for differentiation as 'an ongoing project', and most of each weekly meeting was used as 'a workshop discussion of what works'.

In the mathematics department, which had opted to set pupils from Year 7 onwards, the emphasis was on devising a range of tasks appropriate to pupils within each set, using materials from several published schemes. The year's work had been planned in some detail for each set, with targets based on the Graded Assessment in Maths (GAIM) scheme (Brown, 1992). This ranged from Level 6 for the top sets to Level 2/3 for Set 5. Moreover, the topics within each of the Attainment Targets had been annotated with relevant resources and a range of suggested teaching styles. The head of department said that further materials were being produced at staff workshops, in order to challenge pupils to apply different mathematical skills. In this school, a proposal had to be made annually to the Senior Management Team (SMT) for curriculum bids to support departmental work, and providing extension materials was now a departmental priority. The department had prepared a booklet for governors which was used as the basis for a talk explaining their departmental approach to differentiation. This included a page on planning for differentiation (see Figure 4.3). The booklet also explained that another aspect of the approach was to include a range of teaching styles – individualised learning, class teaching (... 'whole class work allows for discussion and sharing of ideas as an aid to learning'), investigations, project work and the use of computers.

In nearby *River High* school, differentiation in history was strongly resource-based: the Year 7 curriculum had been differentiated in 1993/94, with materials available lesson by lesson, in which aims, objectives and content were clearly set out. In an effort to improve differentiation – that is, to ensure that the needs of all pupils could be met – class teachers had been provided with detailed options to apply to their pupils. In this school, departmental planning for differentiation was being steered towards a common approach, with strong support from the Learning Support team (see Chapter 5). The impetus behind the approach was to ensure that the curriculum was accessible to all, particularly those with learning difficulties; there was also a growing emphasis on the more able. In each department

Figure 4.3:   Excerpt from mathematics department booklet, *Rock High*

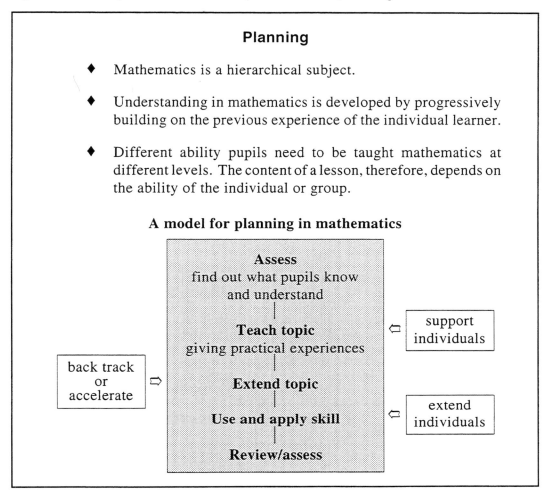

or faculty there was a designated learning support co-ordinator, one of whose responsibilities was curriculum development:

> To assist in the department's programme of introducing and reviewing differentiation within Schemes of Work and associated resourcing.

There was a common programme of target-setting and review involving the faculty co-ordinators and the Learning Support team, but some faculties were making fuller use of this system than others. Developing differentiated work schemes tended to be the first step in a lengthy process of professional development in differentiation; as the science team recommended, 'all differentiated work [to be] shown to all science teachers for comment. This raises awareness for all science teachers and the need to consider this sector of pupils [i.e. those with SEN].' In 1994-95 the focus in most departments was on specific needs of low ability pupils (e.g. in the maths department there were 'an increasing number of children below National Curriculum Level 4') and, in some cases, of the more able (e.g. in science).

In each of these schools, despite the differences of approach, one common element was the requirement to plan schemes of work to meet National Curriculum criteria. In that sense, even senior staff were working within a 'top-down' framework. While this could be perceived as a constraint, this was not always the case. At *Lake High,* the art department said that the advent of the National Curriculum had caused them to implement a tighter scheme of work with explicit criteria. This aimed to ensure that each pupil was able to develop his or her own potential and also allowed teachers to plot the progress of individual pupils adequately. The three teachers within this department all contributed to the development of this scheme of work. This approach is interesting because it was felt to be driven by individual needs and the desire to develop potential. This may be easier in a subject which is not so content based as other foundation subjects.

What was noticeable about these secondary schools was the concerted effort to incorporate differentiation into departmental planning. Indeed, a comparison of their practice with the survey responses suggests that the case-study schools were probably exceptional in the generally high level of staff involvement in strategic planning.

The most easily identified approach to planning for differentiation, especially in the more content-loaded subjects, was the preparation of different 'levels' of pupil materials, especially worksheets, for a given topic. The most common pattern was to plan for three levels, and departmental approaches were in the main concerned with this, devising both schemes of work and materials suitable for these three levels. The work involved in preparing these materials was extensive, and in some cases had clearly benefited from the contribution of the Learning Support staff, in the simplification of language. 'Differentiating' a course was a costly business, in professional effort and materials. The risk was that so much energy could be used up on resource preparation that rather little was left for planning how materials might be used or reviewing how effective they had proved. One example of built-in evaluation for materials was provided at *Lake High*: science revision sheets had been developed for every topic, with graded questions to work through; the reward for this investment was an average increase of two grades between 'mock' and actual GCSE exams.

There seemed to be an assumption in several of the case-study schools that the particular responsibility of the class teacher, in planning for differentiation, was indeed the interpretation of the departmental scheme for the pupils in that class. Where the pupils had already been grouped by ability into sets, the scheme often provided further guidance, explicit or implicit, about the materials, pace or approach to be used. What was less often available were structured ideas and support on just how to adapt or select the material for mixed ability classes. We shall look at the ways in which class teachers organised their learning activities with differentiation in mind in the next section (4.3).

Planning for differentiation in Key Stage 2

All the evidence on planning for differentiation in primary schools comes from the case studies, since the way planning was organised was found to depend very much on the size of the school and its ethos, making a case-study approach more appropriate than survey questions.

In the larger case-study primary schools, curriculum co-ordinators for subjects tended to work with groups of teachers who were responsible for teaching the same age groupings. Curriculum planning usually involved weekly planning sessions as well as longer term planning. Planning for differentiation was related to whole-school policies on pupil grouping. Where the decision had been taken to group pupils by ability for some of the curriculum, this was reflected in planning sessions. However, teachers were concerned first of all with ensuring that they were covering National Curriculum requirements in their plans. The need for learning to match individual needs was a factor in the planning process at some of the case-study schools in these ways:

♦ the fundamental design of schemes of work, aimed to maximise individual development;

♦ the production of differentiated materials;

♦ the decision to utilise particular pupil groupings.

The situation at *Lighthouse Primary* is an example of a common approach to planning seen at other primary schools. Planning at the upper junior stage was carried out by all Year 5 and Year 6 teachers together for the four classes taught by them. The first priority was to ensure that all the relevant National Curriculum Programmes of Study were covered by the time these pupils left the school. A term's plan was drawn up by the year leader and the group met weekly to devise a week's lessons. The year leader liaised with subject co-ordinators concerning subject content, although the staff who were interviewed said that their first point of reference was the National Curriculum documents.

The subject co-ordinator was expected to provide assistance and suggestions for teaching topics. The overall concern here was for curriculum coverage at the planning level, although staff felt that it was important to discuss the suitability of topics and activities for the differing ability ranges at this stage.

Another approach to planning was governed by the grouping systems within year groups. At one junior school (*Windmill Primary*) the Year 4 teachers had divided the two Year 4 classes into five ability groups for reading, within an open-plan area. The two teachers responsible for these classes concentrated on different groups: one took the top and bottom groups, the other one took the three middle groups. In this way it was possible to spend six weeks on phonics with the lowest group, while the top group worked on interpretation of texts. Planning therefore centred on deciding what subject material and activities were the most suitable for these groups. Classroom grouping was the impetus here for addressing needs at the planning stage, as teachers needed to be clear about the focus of tasks and materials for these groupings. This situation was mirrored on a much broader scale in *Abbey Primary* where there were three classes in each year of Key Stage 2. The classes were divided into at least three ability groupings and work in the core subjects was planned for the three groups in the team's weekly planning meetings. Here there was a twin focus: ensuring some teaching by subject specialists (who, it was felt, would more readily be able to meet the needs of able pupils) as well as planning for groups of differing abilities.

At *Cottage Primary*, the small rural primary, planning for the teaching of 26 pupils within the four-year age span across Key Stage 2 had to be detailed and precise and was more closely focused on individual needs at the planning stage. The two teachers, each with a class covering a whole key stage, had to be largely responsible for their own class. However, whole-school topics were planned together and there was an ongoing process of critical review and planning: 'monitoring children's work and planning from that knowledge is a constantly continuing process'. Work for pupils to cover was decided on at a group level, that is there were no overt individual learning plans, but planning was undertaken with levels for individuals in mind. The teacher planned the tasks for her class and the order in which they would undertake them. This was necessary in order for her to know and plan what tasks and what groups she would concentrate on at a particular time. The class activities were therefore timetabled so that the class teacher could efficiently use her time to introduce new topics and monitor the tasks at hand. This head teacher claimed that careful planning enabled her to give maximum attention to individual needs.

This school was exceptional in the detailed planning of content and pre-planned development of pupils' independent learning skills, which were seen as essential to the management of learning. More commonly, although there was a stronger tradition of team planning in primaries, at the level of choosing suitable materials, there was the same tension as in secondary schools about team planning and each teacher's autonomy in their own classroom. One SENCO, who was also a Year 3 class teacher, felt that more systematic development was needed to plan for differentiation. In her view, at present the senior management team did the overall topic cycle planning, working out the targets and what should be covered, but not how.

> The SMT are reviewing the planning sheets to make them more detailed and to force the teacher to think harder about individual needs at the planning stage. Within the same range of work there will have to be ways of tackling it at different levels, and note taken of the resources that will be needed. Some teachers are better at this than others at the moment.

Nonetheless, some teachers were well aware of the fact that it was their expertise in interpreting the planned approaches at classroom level that made differentiation effective, and were glad to accept that responsibility. One Year 4 teacher said that in science she appreciated the element of team planning which allowed her to 'approach it in her own way'. One Year 3 team leader said, 'the strength of our system is that we plan as a team and deliver as individuals'. This suggested that teachers' individual planning was seen as a means of facilitating the real work of interaction between child and teacher, but left open the question of the resources and expertise that schools needed to provide to ensure that all their staff could plan effectively for all their pupils. For the head at this school, planning, whether for the class or for groups, was only one part of the task: 'You can plan till the cows come home, but the bottom line is, do the teachers know their children?' In fact, it was as a result of the two Year 4 teachers reviewing individual needs and progress in reading that they had devised a grouping system for reading, based on reading scores, for two half-mornings a week.

The basis for planning: curriculum needs and pupil needs

Given the universal conviction that 'knowing the pupils' was at the heart of effective differentiation, and that primary teachers in particular valued the opportunities they had to develop a close knowledge of all the children in their class, it is interesting to note how little attention was given to the contribution which formal assessment information could make to the planning process, especially at departmental or team level. Planning was more likely to start from the normative – what an average/above average/below average pupil can do – or from generalised experience of the school intake than from analysis of performance for specific year groups or classes.. It was fairly common to plan for 'types' of pupils, usually defined by ability, or more specifically by competence in handling written texts; or to ensure that a range of teaching approaches and resources were available on which teachers could draw. At team or departmental level, we found that the incidence of 'planning learning to match individual pupils' needs' was low. It only occasionally involved discussion on the suitability of teaching materials and activities for individual pupils, usually those with special needs, in the context of a systematic Learning Support system, as in *Rock High* and *River High*; or in team planning meetings at *Abbey Primary*, where they would plan a task and then discuss how the less able could cope.

This task, of planning to match individual needs, was more usually devolved to classroom level, on the assumption – by no means always realistic – that the class teacher would know the pupils well enough to relate the general plan accurately to those pupils. So the planners – whether subject specialists or teacher teams – generally followed the long-established professional pattern of curriculum development, which usually starts by drawing up a curriculum plan (what to teach) and ends by assessing performance against the plan. It was unlikely, given the dominance of this mode of planning, that teachers adapting the plan for their own classrooms would somehow switch to a very different approach, which starts with assessment information of all kinds and adapts the materials and teaching methods accordingly in order to enable all the pupils to achieve agreed learning goals. There was little evidence that teachers were working in this way. Moreover, many classroom teachers felt under as much pressure as their leaders to ensure their pupils satisfied National Curriculum requirements, as well as the departmental or team specifications.

For newly qualified teachers, in particular, the task of planning with the needs of individuals in mind could be too challenging, as one thoughtful maths probationer at *Rock High* explained:

> I am unsure to what extent I 'plan learning to meet individual needs', although I plan to make sure that everybody has something to do and is stretched. I tend to think in terms of groups or categories of pupils, for example the extent to which they can read. .....I tend to think in relation to whether most pupils can or can't do things, and then think about those who can't.

How could an effective bridge be made between the design of 'differentiated' schemes of work and planning for differentiation at classroom level? From the case-study evidence, the indications are that this depended crucially on professional teamwork – regular departmental or team meetings, sessions with the SENCO, team-teaching or observation of each other's classes.

In the case-study schools, insistence upon regular team or departmental meetings was thought by teachers to aid the development of differentiation in these ways:

♦ it enabled staff to consider jointly the best ways of presenting elements of the programme of study and give them the opportunity to gain the perspectives of other colleagues on the suitability and range of tasks or teaching materials;

♦ it created the means for staff to be reflective about their methods and techniques and to receive views and advice from other colleagues.

In other words, it was the ongoing review of classroom planning and its practical outcomes which did most to develop the necessary expertise for putting principles into practice.

4.3 Practising Differentiation

Whatever the level of support at departmental or year group level in the planning stage, and whatever decisions had been made by senior or middle managers about pupil grouping, each teacher had to decide how to manage the learning process to maximise progress for pupils in the classes s/he taught. By using the common framework in the case-study schools to ask teachers what strategies they used, combined with observing them in use, and setting these findings in the context of teachers' perceptions obtained through the national survey, we hoped to build up a balanced picture of practice. To introduce this section, we shall look first at the overview provided by the national survey findings. These were obtained, it will be remembered, from primary heads (who were asked to consult with all their Key Stage 2 staff in order to present a consensus view) and from heads of English, maths and science (who were similarly asked to consult with departmental colleagues). All these respondents were presented with a list of differentiation strategies and asked how practicable they found each one for meeting pupils' individual learning needs.

Figure 4.4: Percentage of teachers 'generally' using certain differentiation strategies with Key Stage 2 or Key Stage 3 teachers

Primary heads and teachers

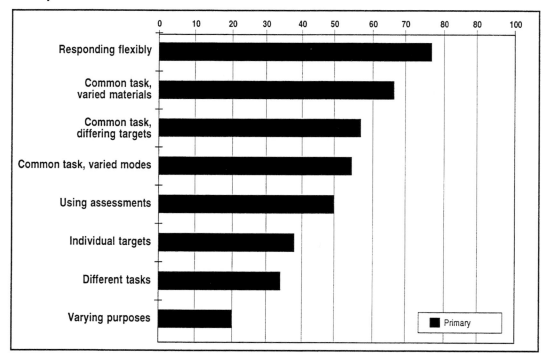

Secondary heads of department

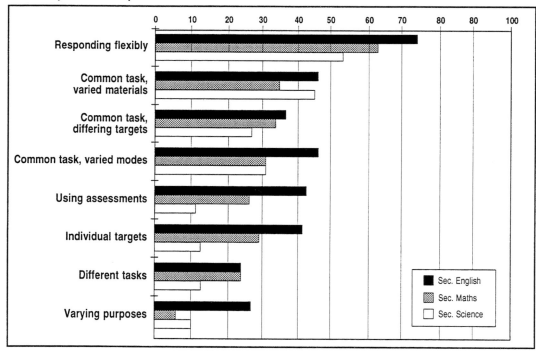

The clearest result in the figure is that the strategy most likely to be 'generally' used, by all groups, was the 'flexible response'. This was also the only one in this list presented in the survey which dealt mainly with teachers' response while teaching. All the others involved some form of pre-planning, of materials or goals. The other striking pattern is that primary teachers were much more likely than secondary colleagues to say they 'generally' used some of these approaches. Over half of them reported that they generally planned a common topic with a variety of learning materials, differing learning targets or response modes and exactly 50 per cent said they generally used assessments to plan individual targets. Among the secondary specialists, the English teachers seemed nearer to this pattern than the other two core subjects. Science departments, the least likely to find it practicable to relate learning to individual assessments or targets, were similar to their English colleagues in offering a variety of materials for the common task (about 45 per cent 'generally' did this).

Further analyses showed that there were two dimensions or factors underlying this list of strategies. The first focused on varying the work within a *common frame*; it was defined mainly by the three items above linked to a common task, although most items had some link to it. The second dimension was related to setting *individual targets* and brought together that item with the use of assessment. On each of these underlying factors, the English teachers scored significantly higher – that is they were more likely than teachers in the other two subjects to claim they were using this type of approach; maths teachers were more likely than science teachers to be targeting learning to individuals.

However, it must be remembered that these are teachers' reports, in the constrained context of a questionnaire, which is inevitably a rather blunt instrument for investigating the process of classroom learning. This is why we have focused here on relative differences between teacher groups and between strategies rather than absolute percentages, which as we shall see in reviewing the case-study evidence, seem to present a rather optimistic picture of classroom practice. What these results do suggest is that there were systematic variations in teachers' perceptions about the strategies that they felt were practicable to meet individual needs in the classroom.

The case studies allowed us to explore teachers' views more flexibly, as well as setting them alongside classroom observations. Most find it fairly hard to select and prioritise the strategies they used; some said 'we use them all'. In presenting this evidence, we shall look first at the strategies which involved some form of pre-planning by the teacher. This includes most of those listed in Figure 4.4. Secondly, we review the responsive strategies which teachers use in the course of teaching and learning. This will also cover some discussion of how teachers respond to the different speeds at which pupils complete essentially common tasks.

Pre-planned strategies

We have seen that, even when there was detailed team planning of schemes of work, it still remained the responsibility of each teacher to achieve the desired match between the agreed learning objectives and the pupils in each class. In doing this, perhaps the most important factor was how well the teacher knew the pupils (survey findings on this issue are discussed in Chapter 5). What did this mean in practice? And how was the knowledge used for lesson preparation?

Using knowledge about pupils: assessment and target-setting. Teachers of all types of pupils consistently stressed that it was the knowledge that they built up about pupils as they dealt with them in the classroom that was mostly likely to influence the way they planned for matching individual learning needs. One Year 5 teacher said 'I get to a point with each child when I know when to skip things.' It is this informal use of continuous assessment that the majority of teachers interviewed aimed at. A secondary school teacher told a researcher about a Year 8 French class, 'I can't start differentiating yet, I don't them well enough.' Plenty of pupil records existed for this teacher's information but she still felt that she needed to plan on the basis of her own knowledge gained through classroom interaction.

It seemed to the research team that practising teachers perceived informal assessment very differently from the formal assessments they were required to record at certain times of the school year. A constant theme in interviews was that it was very difficult for them to manage and digest the amount of information available about pupils in school's formal record systems. On the other hand, a history teacher from *River High*, with departmental responsibility for learning support and some years' involvement in differentiation, regretted the lack of specific information from assessments, for 'the great mass of pupils. Only the form teacher has access to very personal information.'

Most teachers felt that they needed to operate a diagnostic period, either formally or informally, for part of the first half term of teaching the group. In taking over a class from a colleague within the school, this often seemed to mean relying more on personal observation and discussion than on any written records. Indeed, some teachers preferred to start with a 'blank sheet'. One Year 5 teacher explained her reluctance to use the Year 4 reading test results of her pupils because she felt that the test was outdated but said she felt proficient in her own assessment of reading. She had also used pupils' reports to gain extra information about pupils. In her view, the most useful source, however, was the person who had taught these pupils last year. The school arranged for these two teachers to liaise and consult about the transfer of pupils.

Even when schools had developed systems to promote the use of target-setting this did not always seem to help teachers to 'know their pupils', in relation to their learning needs. A number of schools had established processes whereby class teachers were involved in discussing individual learning targets with pupils as part of a profiling system such as Records of Achievement. Other teachers conducted regular dialogue with pupils which aimed to review progress and plan future development. However, target-setting undertaken with pupils often seemed to be an 'extra', with targets being chosen or expressed by the pupils in general terms (I must improve my spelling/the presentation of my work) and not in a form which could feed directly into lesson plans.

At one high school *(Hillside High)* the English department felt that the school's Integrated Curriculum Assessment, a cross-curricular monitoring system of motivation and achievement, enabled teachers to engage in reviews of pupils' progress. Assessors (the pupil's subject teachers) provided a grade from 1-4 on each of nine areas: general attitudes, attendance, punctuality to lessons, personal organisation, homework, learning work, understanding, ability to apply information learned, conduct. A sheet had to be completed for each child at the end of every work unit. In some teachers' view, such a system caused manageability problems and the tendency was to use it in a summative, rather than a formative manner.

A rather different approach being developed in several primary schools was to develop a bank of actual pupil assignments to represent performance at a specific level. This was being built up through a moderation process. At *Abbey Primary* 'every year group has an English profile with details of the activity input, how much help was given and then a class list of who did and didn't achieve and examples of work which achieved different levels'. But the issue remained, how was such material actually used by teachers?

What teachers seemed to require, as a foundation, was to become acquainted with their pupils as learners. Once they had achieved this level of knowledge, it seemed, they felt they could plan the class's work effectively. Some teachers, particularly those with primary classes, might then develop detailed analyses of pupils' performance which would feed into their planning. The survey suggested, however, that using assessment information to plan learning targets for most pupils, however, remained the exception. Figure 4.5 shows the proportion of each group of survey respondents who said that they used assessment to plan individual targets.

The diagram shows that although there were some primary schools and secondary departments who claimed routinely to use assessment to plan individual targets, there was a majority who only did so 'sometimes' (between one-quarter and one-third), 'occasionally' (a variable proportion), or never (17 per cent of science staff, but less than 10 per cent of other groups).

Figure 4.5:   Differentiation strategies: use of assessments to plan individual targets

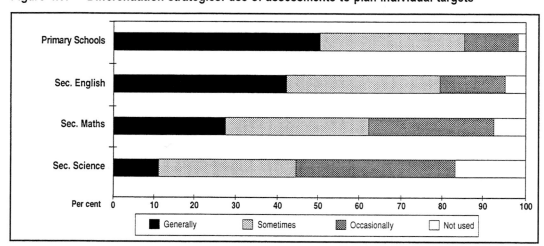

For the majority of secondary teachers, therefore, and half of the Key Stage 2 staff, this was not the expected basis for organising most pupils' work, a finding borne out by the interviews with many of the teachers in the case-study schools. It was most likely to occur in structured teaching schemes, for example in maths. Thus in *Hillside High* and *Rock High*, maths booklets were allocated to match pupil performance in tests.

What emerges from the case studies is that most teachers did not base their differentiation strategies mainly on systematic diagnostic assessment and individual target setting, but rather that they adapted their curriculum plans in some respects, as they got to know their pupils in class, to fit their perceived strengths and weaknesses. Knowledge of the latter was based above all on personal classroom experience, supplemented by discussion with other teachers and, where it seemed relevant, by assessment information – test scores, National Curriculum levels and school reports.

We have seen, however, that many departments and teams in the case-study schools had anticipated the need to meet a wide range of abilities in their strategic planning and that at this level the planning was based broadly on pupil types – most typically three levels of ability. In these schools and departments, teachers were expecting and indeed prepared to provide some variation of experience, within a common framework; their task was to decide how their pupils matched these types so that they could use the resources or approaches to best effect. We therefore looked at the way classroom work was structured; to what extent all pupils were expected to undertake the same task, using the same resources, in the same time-frame, and how and why the experience was differentiated.

In-class support. In the case-study schools extensive use was made both of teachers and of adults other than teachers to provide in-class support, ranging from learning support assistants (LSAs) to parents who would assist the teacher in helping pupils with their reading. The most systematic use of LSAs was found in two of the secondary schools whose learning support structures are described more fully in Chapter 5. In both schools the LSAs received structured support and training and worked as a team with the head of department or co-ordinator. Further details are given below of how the system worked in one of these schools.

> At *River High* there was a team of six paid LSAs who were trained to work in class, where they worked with up to eight pupils, with close liaison with the subject teacher. This was in addition to full-time support for the 12 statemented pupils. They were given a Learning Support Handbook as well as ongoing training. One of the LSAs explained how she sometimes worked with specific pupils, for example in a lower set for Year 9 history, supporting seven pupils; and at other times offering whole-class support in Year 7 maths (again, a lower set). In other classes she had found that some bright girls asked for help. Once a week she talked with pupils about their personal targets, negotiating with the teacher on the basis of the departmental target bank. Although some targets were too 'bland', teachers themselves learned from working with the LSAs. She felt they had respect from teachers and from pupils and explained how she had 'negotiated' with a teacher on behalf of one of the boys she was supporting. She saw herself as responsible for helping with individuals, while the teacher was in charge of the whole class. 'It is a delicate role knowing when to step on the pupils and not tread on their toes.' She was well aware of the school's approach to differentiation and felt they were making progress. 'Ultimately we are aiming to make pupils more able to support themselves. Some come on in leaps and bounds... others have found a strategy of learned helplessness.'

At *Windmill Primary* there were seven LSAs, each for one designated (statemented) pupil, but the SENCO explained that in practice she worked with a number of pupils in the class. In addition, some (secondary) subject teachers offered in-class support within their departments and this was included in their job descriptions. This was most effective where the department was already working closely as a team, with an 'open door' policy between classrooms. The key issue for all support staff was whether the class or subject teacher had planned the work with them beforehand, so that roles and specific goals were clear. Unfortunately, this was certainly not always the case. Other forms of in-class support were on offer in some schools.

> At *Lake High*, where about 22 per cent of the intake was of minority ethnic origin (mainly Pakistani), there was also funding for teaching English and providing in-class support for those not yet fluent in English. Two subject teachers (English and science) were providing such support and five of the LSAs spoke Urdu/Punjabi. Given the policy of integrating pupils with English as a second (or third) language fully into ordinary classes, they had to allocate the support to the classes with the largest number of beginners. They could use materials prepared by the co-ordinator and her team, and these were also available to other classes. The aim was to encourage collaborative learning (getting native speakers to work with bilingual pupils) and partnership teaching – full co-operation between language support staff and subject teachers. The language support team had produced a language policy document to encourage these processes, and a full list of all bilingual pupils, listing (and explaining) the stage of English language learning they had reached.

In-class support was more closely focused in schools such as *Hillside High* and *Abbey Primary* where pupils with SEN were taught in separate classes, at least for core subjects. At *Hillside High* it was possible to provide a higher staffing ratio for these classes, of teachers and LSAs, and to offer specific initiatives such as the paired reading project in Year 7. One consequence of this approach was that it could be difficult to provide sufficient support for sets just above this level.

All the schools were in the process of implementing their policies to meet the requirements of the SEN Code of Practice; one aspect of this was guidance to teachers on managing pupils who had been referred as 'Stage 1', according to the criteria of the Code, whether or not any additional support was available. In response to such a referral, the Learning Advice Department at *Lake High* provided the teacher with a planning record for each such student, indicating the strategies which they felt might be helpful and asking the teacher to keep a running record of the strategies they actually used. These are shown in the box, and are usefully specific.

Subject teacher's planning record for Stage 1 students

Extra explanation/instruction

Differentiate material

Adapt task

Encourage student to work with others

Check homework is recorded in diary

Record homework in diary for student

Student to write spellings on Word Coupons

Student to record punctuation errors

Discuss student's work with tutor

Commend work with Praise Stickers

Adapt medium of work (writing to speaking)

Learning structure. We have seen that the survey suggested that at least one-third of teachers 'generally' presented the class with a common topic or task, with the variation designed to meet pupils' differing capabilities introduced as the topic was developed. In fact, two-thirds or more did this either 'generally' or 'sometimes'. These responses leave it unclear whether, on other occasions, the common topic was or was not differentiated in this way. What the lesson observations indicated was that, certainly in Key Stage 3, the most common pattern for lessons observed in all subject disciplines was to start with a common core stimulus or task. This pattern was also true of some Key Stage 2 sessions. These lessons began with a whole class explanation, followed by all pupils being set one or more activities, to work on individually or (less often) collaboratively. However, the way in which these activities were structured, and the level of self-management which pupils were expected to display varied considerably.

Even in these schools which were focusing on differentiation, there were examples of lessons with very little evidence of planned variation to meet learning needs. A Year 9 History lesson seemed to typify this approach. The teacher gave a whole class introduction about the slave trade and then pupils were asked to undertake the same worksheet and tasks. A lower set Year 9 geography lesson presented pupils with a single worksheet to work on, following the initial discussion; here the assumption was that the pre-selection had already occurred through setting. A very common pattern for mathematics, foreshadowed in the previous section, was exemplified in one of the case-study secondary schools, where the pupils all followed the same topic but groups of pupils undertook different tasks at different levels, as defined in the departmental scheme of work. But the same basic lesson structure could be carefully structured to provide not only varied levels of worksheet but also opportunities for all to participate fully in discussion. Two lessons with one Year 7 English class showed how all members of a mixed ability class could be fully and appropriately engaged in the same task. In the second lesson on communication, the initial discussion, to which all could contribute, was followed by an exercise in using hieroglyphics which used the same format, but presented it more explicitly for those needing support, while providing sufficient challenge for the most able pupils.

Sometimes the common stimulus was followed by a task with more opportunities for pupils to shape their response, using a range of materials. A science lesson at Year 6 contained a core task where all the pupils were required to design an effective seed-emitting structure. After ten minutes' introduction the pupils were instructed to start the task by choosing equipment and referring to resource books for ideas. They were provided with a range of resources and pupils worked within friendship groups but at an individual pace. The majority of pupils engaged in the task for twenty minutes doing their experiments. Some disaffection was observed, especially amongst those who found it difficult to decide on their experiment. The class was drawn together after half an hour for a discussion about what they had learnt through the experiment. The challenge here was to provide differentiated guidance to ensure that all the members of each group could meet the basic criterion, that their experiment was capable of testing their hypothesis. Pre-planning this guidance called for considerable professional experience and expertise about possible responses and the understanding, knowledge and attitudes pupils were bringing to the task.

The teacher of a Year 9 English class, set to work in groups on preparing a guide to the school for new pupils, seemed to be aware of these needs, offering very different levels of guidance to each group. In this case, however, the 'common stimulus' pattern was extended over a unit of work covering a number of lessons, and the task they were carrying out offered a range of opportunities for differentiation.

Lessons which started with a common task followed by some variation in resources or methods were seen in science, mathematics, English, French and geography at secondary level and at primary level in mathematics, humanities and science.

As soon as variations of some type are planned into the lesson, a whole number of classroom management issues arise. On the one hand, there were many instances of teacher direction, where pupils were expected to use worksheets or other resources of a pre-specified *level*, perhaps within pre-specified groups. Alternatively, most pupils might start with the same resources and task, only a minority working with simpler materials, with more challenging options kept as extension work for those completing the main task. In a geography department, which had recently introduced work at three levels, it appeared that the higher level task was often retained in this way as an extension task; by contrast, English teachers at *Rock High* were trying to provide extension materials at each level. Some maths teachers were developing problems which would challenge pupils in a different way, by encouraging them to apply a wider range of mathematical skills. These moves to develop the idea of 'extension' work, beyond the rather limited idea of 'something for the more able' or (not always the same thing) 'those who finish quickly', were a useful expansion of the 'challenge' strategy, to encourage all pupils to go a bit further than the core task required, perhaps to use learning methods that were less familiar.

It was important to be clear about the purpose of introducing variations to the common task, and the role of teacher and pupils in deciding what approach should be used. Where the purpose was primarily *challenge*, the teacher usually directed the pupils fairly closely. On the other hand, some variations seemed to be designed to offer a diversity of activities or methods to increase motivation and (possibly) foster pupils' capacity to manage their own learning; if so, then pupils were more likely to be invited to choose. One English lesson about *Midsummer Night's Dream* involved pupils making their own choice of activity from a list on the blackboard. These activities included watching a video, acting out a scene, filling in worksheets or drawing some of the characters. This range of choice was unusual in secondary classrooms. It could be said to foster differentiation in that it enabled pupils to practise a higher degree of independence by choosing tasks which would help them to learn effectively. However, there is the possibility in these circumstances of pupils always choosing tasks which present the least challenge, a risk of which the teacher of this class was well aware.

The problems relating to choice and challenge arose more often in Key Stage 2 classrooms, where the core task pattern was more difficult to discern because of the way the day was ordered. Time spans for tasks were often longer, with a number of tasks relating to different subject areas on hand during the day. Although the greater flexibility which this structure offered could be used to adjust the task for individuals, considerable experience and skill was needed by the teacher to maintain an appropriate level of challenge for all the pupils. In at least some of these classrooms, increasing choice and diversity seemed sometimes to be seen as a desirable end in itself. For some pupils, choice presented problems and was not apparently enhancing learning. A higher ability (Level 4) Year 6 pupil at *Lighthouse Primary*, who had been asked to do some extension work relating to war leaders in the second world war, spent most of the morning looking vainly for relevant resource books, in the classroom and the library. Later in the morning, she admitted she had found nothing, and was filling in time before turning to a related practical activity.

Sometimes SEN pupils were given work which was so different from the work being done by the rest of the class that it was hard to see it as part of a common task or topic, or designed to reach a common learning goal. There was undoubtedly a tension here between providing equality of access to the curriculum, even if this seemed to mean carrying out low-level activities in the same content area, and designing work appropriate to the individual's needs. Maintaining a common framework was seen as important by many teachers, either from principle or because the scheme of work had been structured in this way. The variations depended to some extent on whether in-class support was available. But prior planning of resources was also vital. In one science department, the deputy learning support co-ordinator explained how they were building up a glossary of scientific terms, simply explained, for every module, and discussed how certain worksheet questions could be undertaken more effectively through peer tutoring. At schools such as *Abbey Primary* and *Hillside High*, where the least able were in special groups for at least the core subjects, then the pressure to maintain a common learning structure was greatly reduced and activities seen as appropriate (such as paired reading) introduced.

The national picture, as monitored by teachers' responses in the survey, was of a largely common programme for all pupils. The proportion of respondents saying that they planned different topics or tasks for some pupils was low, both in the case-study schools and in the survey. Only 34 per cent of primary school heads mentioned that they regularly used this strategy, whilst this figure was less for both mathematics and English respondents (23 per cent) and 12 per cent for science teachers. This survey data confirms the evidence gained from the case-study interviews and observations that teachers predominantly use a common learning structure, more especially at secondary level.

Resources. The availability of a range of resources can enable pupils to focus more effectively on the task at hand and foster pupils' learning by encouraging greater interest and independence. But it was clear from the case studies that providing a variety of resources was not in itself likely to enhance learning, unless the resources were appropriate for task and pupils, and pupils had been taught how to manage them.

During lessons at *Abbey Primary,* pupils were able to access a wide range of resources from an adjacent resource area. At *Lighthouse Primary* teachers felt that they would not be able to offer differentiated activities without pupils being able to readily make use of a wide range of resources. The resource areas of all the classrooms had been very carefully and systematically laid out to ensure that pupils knew exactly where to find things even if they changed classes or rooms. Staff hoped this would increase their independence and give them a sense of responsibility for keeping their own resources tidy. At *Cottage Primary*, pupils were taught to organise their own learning resources from an early age.

A number of Key Stage 2 lessons were seen, especially in science, where greater pupil responsibility and independence was fostered through the use of relevant resources. In these lessons teachers had to ensure that pupils could draw on a wide range of resources in order for them to carry out their tasks at an appropriate pace and level of ability. In one Year 6 science lesson, pupils were required to decide upon and undertake an experiment of their own choice. The teacher provided a number of books which contained experiments. These books were used by a quarter of the class, the other pupils had devised their own experiments. In order to set up their experiments pupils were required to gather together the necessary equipment from classroom storerooms or other places in school, including outdoors and in the school playground. The higher ability pupils were able to deal well with collecting equipment and conducting the experiment, but there was need of much support at this stage for the groups of middle and lesser ability students. It was when the more able pupils needed to record their conclusions and test their hypothesis that the focus was switched to these pupils by the teacher. The teacher was capable of engaging the higher level pupils by acting as a mentor to promote further understanding in the subject discipline.

One of the most innovative use of resources was the use of laptops to aid differentiation. *Observatory Primary* school had been supplied with a number of laptops and an integrated software package which developed pupils' IT skills and also their ability to think carefully about the nature of tasks and their presentation. The class teacher felt that that differentiation was built into this situation, in that the most able were able to extend themselves as they were naturally inquisitive and were keen to acquire knowledge. He felt that the middle range of pupils required more intervention, support and monitoring of outcome. The perceived benefits of the extensive usage of laptops were that they helped to develop listening skills, improve concentration on task and encouraged pupils to ask for help. As examples given in Chapter 3 showed, the laptops also actively encouraged peer tutoring.

Nonetheless, the majority of lessons observed, particularly in Key Stage 3, revealed a mixed approach to the use of resources, with teachers most commonly depending upon prepared worksheets or course books. The development, storage and management of printed resources, computer software and other media designed to meet a variety of pupil needs was a major challenge, and often was only accomplished with sustained support and dedicated time for collaboration between subject specialists and learning support staff. Even those schools which were seen to be most committed to differentiation were aware of very uneven development across departments in building up resource banks that would enable all pupils to access the curriculum and/or extend their learning. Even more importantly, there were few indications of Key Stage 3 pupils being taught to develop the skills needed to use resources independently. Providing a range of resources to promote differentiation was clearly not enough; either pupils were to remain dependent on the teacher for guidance in their use, or pupils had to be taught how to select what was appropriate to their needs. One way of doing this, in addition to subject-based teaching, was to create a professionally managed resource centre. At *River High* they had invested £20,000 over three years in a resource-based learning centre, which provided practical help on an individual basis, both in class and by pupils coming to the centre. It had developed extension packs to provide additional interest.

Pupil management. The one, taken-for-granted assumption for any school is that pupils are taught in classes, and that therefore the way they are organised for work within the class, whether individually or collaboratively, is a key aspect of the teacher's own differentiation strategy. Some factors were outside the teacher's control. For example, decisions about setting or banding were often taken by senior managers (or sometimes middle managers) and will be reviewed in Chapter 5. However, in primary schools, as we have seen in this chapter, year teams had more say in arrangements for setting, usually in the core subjects, and were certainly creating these groups as part of their differentiation strategy.

Within their classes, teachers grouped their pupils for work in a various ways, including friendship groups, ability groups, age groups, groups by task, and pupil-chosen groups. Pupils were more likely to be grouped according to friendship groups, or allowed to choose their own groups, if they had already been placed in sets or other ability groupings. Some teachers felt that pupil setting had already created differentiation and this did not need to be carried further by arranging ability groupings within the set.

Although pupils were often placed in groups by teachers, the extent of group collaborative work observed was limited, especially in the secondary schools. There the tendency was to set tasks for pairs, rather than larger groups; or, more often, to set tasks for pupils to work at individually, whatever the seating arrangements. In the lessons which used a common core activity, there was more whole class teaching and pair work. If the teacher provided a variety of activities or approaches then pupils usually had to be organised into a number of working groups. In some cases, this was planned to implement a differentiated structure. In *Abbey Primary* the class teacher was responsible for teaching her own class for the term's topic of Ancient Egyptians. For other subjects the class would have been divided into ability groups across the year group, that is, pupils would be taught with others of the same ability by one of the three teachers in that year group. For the topic sessions, the class teacher arranged pupils to sit in groups according to ability. Each group was set different tasks and the most able group was given an extension task. The pupils were required to collaborate to gather the necessary information about aspects of Egyptian life.

In the majority of the mathematics lessons observed by the research team pupils worked individually, although they were often seated in groups. The nature of the course books or materials used often appeared to foster individual learning plans. We did not see many mathematics lessons on investigations, which might have contained a higher level of collaborative work. In one Key Stage 2 mathematics lesson pupils were required to work in pairs although they tended to function as individuals as they carried out investigations into number patterns. The tasks were paper-based, requiring the pupils to relate tables to number patterns, and although pupils could co-operate they were being asked to provide results of individual endeavours.

One of the least common strategies used by teachers was varying pupil roles, that is a pupil acting as group chairman, or being involved in role play or acting as a scribe. In one Year 9 English lesson at *Rock High,* two pupils were asked to read out a brief story they had written, and the teacher explained to the rest of the class what was involved in serving as the audience. In another English lesson, for Year 7 at *Lake High,* the whole period was spent on role play, with pupils working in groups. Researchers observed pupils being asked to take on roles such as group leader, or discussion chairman, more often in language lessons, both in secondary and primary schools. Again the issue was one of purpose: were these roles being used to develop particular skills, or as an effective way for these pupils to contribute? Were the pupils taught the skills they needed to function in a variety of roles? At *Cottage Primary,* the head explained, 'we teach group skills here and all the pupils get a turn as group leader – they all need to learn how to stop pushy people, how to plan work or assemblies. Was the pedagogical purpose clear, to teacher and to the pupils? Was their performance monitored? The low usage of varying pupil roles reported in the survey responses suggested that this approach was not widely recognised as relevant to differentiation.

Primary teachers were keen to promote pupil collaboration, and to encourage pupils to learn from one another. But this required expertise. The ability of teachers to co-operate with and deploy other personnel in the classroom – whether teaching colleagues or LSAs – often opened the way for them to consider how to use pupils to provide support for their peers. As we have seen in Chapter 4, other pupils could play an important role. In *Lighthouse Primary* each project group was given a leader and deputy leader, who had a responsibility towards the less able. One Year 6 teacher was provided with an LSA for a pupil who had a range of moderate learning difficulties. When this assistant was not in the class, other pupils functioned in a similar role in ensuring that he understood the task to be undertaken by explaining certain words with which he had difficulty. In the lesson observed by the NFER researcher, a pupil took R's dictation and then together they set about producing a story together. Other teachers who were actively interested in improving the independent learning strategies of their pupils felt there was mutual benefit in this role. One such Year 4 teacher said that he considered pupils to be 'useful tools' in his differentiation strategy. This school (*Lighthouse Primary*) also operated a 'buddy' system where older pupils helped those coming in to Key Stage 2 to find their feet. Another pupil support strategy was in operation in *Observatory Primary* school, at that point still a middle school with Year 7 pupils; they were 'twinned' with the Reception class, and were gaining in confidence as they learned to hear children read.

In Chapter 3 we noted that the survey showed that teachers – particularly Key Stage 3 teachers – were not very confident of their pupils' competence in managing their own learning, and in interviews we found that some teachers exercised a form of differentiation here, only allowing the more able to undertake research or other more challenging roles. More discussion was needed about how teaching pupils to exercise a wider range of roles, and in particular building on their skills in managing their learning through Key Stage 2 and Key Stage 3, might actually help to achieve the underlying goal of raising the achievement of all pupils.

Another way of managing pupils' work was to offer the possibility of alternative *modes of response*. In the survey, just over half (54 per cent) the primary heads said that their teachers generally found it practicable to use a common task with differing response modes as a differentiation strategy. It was not as popular at secondary level, with 46 per cent of heads of English departments mentioning that this strategy was generally used, compared with 31 per cent of the Science and Mathematics departments who responded.

Along with class question and answer sessions, the written response mode was the most common within the lessons we observed, which were predominantly in the three core subjects. However some teachers encouraged pupils to vary the way they responded within this mode, by attempting to stimulate more extended writing. One example of this was a Year 9 Geography lesson where the work was graded from closed comprehension type questions to the presentation of written descriptions.

Some subjects, such as those which are language and design-related, more readily allow pupils to consider how best to respond to the stimulus. In one Year 8 English lesson pupils could produce a story board, answer questions, or conduct a discussion about the poem read by the teacher. In other contexts, teacher direction was thought to be more effective in providing the relevant challenge for pupils. In a Year 10 science lesson at a special school the more able pupils were asked to make models about the topic discussed – the digestive system of the body – whereas those considered not capable of this activity were given more structured tasks, such as drawing or using a computer program.

Again, the important questions were about purpose. Should certain pupils – predominantly those who had problems with literacy – be offered another mode (tape-recording, drawing) to express their ideas, on the same task; or were they really just being kept busy (for example by drawing or colouring)? Was an alternative mode an inappropriate solution, if they needed to be helped to improve their literacy? Just as importantly, were pupils who were competent in written answers being challenged to develop their oral skills? And how important is it to develop pupils' ability to select the response mode they consider most appropriate and effective?

Responsive strategies

Responsive differentiation strategies are defined here as the approaches used by teachers when they respond differentially to pupils during the teaching and learning process. It is quite possible, as has been noted above, that teachers plan to build these differential responses into their lessons, but their actual nature and form will depend on the teachers 'real time' decisions and actions. Teachers will expect to spend some time monitoring and reviewing pupils' progress. What cannot be planned is the way that pupils deal with certain tasks at a particular time, although the repeated use of activities with similar groups under typical conditions will provide the teacher with a reasonable idea of the range of performance to expect. As we saw in Figure 4.4, 'responding flexibly' fitted alongside the lesson structure of 'common task with variations' as the strategies most likely to be seen as practicable.

Figure 4.6 **'Responding flexibly': percentage of teachers using this differentiation strategy**

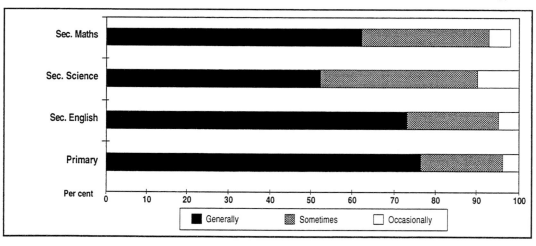

Figure 4.6 shows the survey responses for this item in more detail with secondary English again closely reflecting the primary response. As the figure shows, almost all teachers reported using flexible response as a differentiation strategy at least 'sometimes', and for primary teachers and secondary English teachers about three-quarters 'generally' did so.

We will look now at two aspects of flexible response: interactions with pupils and managing the pace of learning.

Patterns of interaction. Teachers implement differentiation most often in the process of interaction with pupils. But the phrase may have also been interpreted rather flexibly, to cover many types of interaction with individuals and small groups, as well as the more specific interventions targeted at individuals to provide an appropriate challenge, based on detailed knowledge of his or her capacities. Just as most teachers were familiar with the idea of differentiation by outcome, even if they meant by this that a class of pupils would tackle any task with varying degrees of success, so they could nearly all agree that responding flexibly was a regular strategy for differentiation. But is this just a convenient re-labelling of good standard classroom practice? Certainly some teachers thought so, and others argued that differentiation was automatic, just part of normal practice. As one experienced primary assessment co-ordinator, a Key Stage 1 teacher, commented, 'I regard class teachers as doing differentiation "in their heads" as part of their regular practice.' But that was less than helpful to explain the process to less experienced teachers. In practice, their best opportunity to learn was to watch an experienced teacher at work, a system which was actively encouraged in some schools and happened informally in others.

In the *Cottage Primary* classrooms, the class teacher regularly varied the way she talked to pupils in the different ability groups. In particular, she knew which pupils to target and what aspects of their work to focus on. At times, it could appear that she was relentless in the way she questioned and challenged some pupils who tended to make little progress and were reluctant to undertake more challenging tasks. Continued observation and interviews with children revealed that this was necessary to promote maximum performance and was interpreted as such by pupils and parents.

It is possible for this questioning technique to be used effectively in a whole class situation, such as a Year 9 mathematics lesson, when the teacher conducted a quick-fire whole-class session as a preparation for a mini test. In doing this he succeeded in checking their mathematical understanding through oral review of their answers A similar interaction was observed with a Year 9 science lesson which was a review session after the pupils had conducted a practical investigation. The usefulness of this time was slightly jeopardised by one 'attention seeker' who tried to answer more than his share of questions.

It was quite usual for Key Stage 2 teachers in the case-study schools to conduct short review sessions with groups about the activities at hand. This was also the case in a Year 8 English lesson when the teacher moved from group to group, monitoring pupils' discussion about a poem, providing necessary prompts and supplying additional questions to be addressed.

It was not difficult to identify examples of teachers responding flexibly through their questioning of pupils and in many other ways; for example, by directing a child to alternative materials or resources, by managing the pace of work for individuals or groups, or – less commonly – by allocating roles (chairing, reporting back, peer tutoring). It was harder to decide whether the intervention was really fulfilling differentiation principles, as teachers defined them, or serving other purposes, such as classroom control.

However, it seems surprising that in the case-study schools, with their explicit focus on differentiation, researchers recorded a substantial proportion of lessons, especially at secondary level, where there was no flexible questioning.

Whilst this approach may lie at the heart of good teaching, using 'flexible response' to pupils' learning needs as the main differentiation strategy raises other questions. Teachers were often unable to target a wide range of pupils during a lesson. They also had to rely on their knowledge of the class to aid them in deciding which pupils to question, for example with the Year 6 teacher closely directing the work of the individuals within the group. Teachers can sometimes be distracted by those pupils who appear to be more 'needy' than others. From the lesson observations it appeared that teachers' attention, of necessity, was drawn to those who had experienced difficulty or lack of understanding with tasks and it involved considerable classroom management skills to attend appropriately to all pupils. If differentiation is to be effective there is a need for teachers to develop strategies to ensure all pupils are being appropriately challenged. This may only be possible by drawing on other approaches as well – target-setting, greater pupil responsibility for accepting and working towards targets, more planning with LSAs, and use of other adults. Above all, experienced teachers need to analyse and describe what they do, so that their colleagues can more rapidly develop and share these skills.

Judging the pace. We found that teachers at primary level and secondary level regularly take into account the fact that pupils will work at a different *pace* and had prepared additional activities for the faster ones to undertake once they had finished the task at hand. The need to manage the pace of learning, lesson by lesson, was particularly important in subjects or schools with highly structured topic or module frameworks. This was more common in Key Stage 3, but it may be remembered that teachers at *Abbey Primary* were worried about the need to keep their sets in step for topics. Alternatively, most primary class teachers had built a session into their timetables, often on a Friday when pupils would be required to finish work. The locus of control within the classroom determined whether the pupils needed to be told what to do when they finished, or whether, of their own accord, they would start on some new activity. In the majority of lessons observed pupils would either be told, or would ask the teacher, before proceeding to an extension task.

Pupils who finished the common task were regularly provided with, or in the cases where there was greater pupil independence, selected, an extension task, usually from a worksheet or course book. At primary level, class teachers directed pupils to an extension task or some unfinished work when the main activity was completed. This was easier to accomplish if the teacher was responsible for teaching more than one area of the curriculum. Even if the main lesson was based upon the use of common core tasks, secondary teachers might ask pupils to undertake an extension task.

Much depended on the teacher's vigilance in monitoring the class. This was a demanding task. In *Cottage Primary*, the task list for each pupil group ensured that pupils knew what to do next and when to move onto it. However, certain pupils required repeated reminding by the teacher, even when they knew what was expected of them. For example, a middle ability pupil had spent three-quarters of an hour on an English exercise, and some time day-dreaming when it was suggested to him by the teacher that he proceeded to his mathematics task. After five minutes the teacher checked that he had moved on, but he was still on the English exercise. He finally commenced his mathematics ten minutes after being told to consider doing so.

At secondary level, teachers usually attempted to get pupils to finish their work within a given time, often because of the nature of the timed periods of the teaching day. At *Hillside High,* the nature of the modular maths scheme appeared to militate against pupils working at their own pace, as there was a need to complete modules within a specific time. The head of mathematics said, 'In theory there could be a different flow chart route (through the booklets containing subject topics), but in practice there is one [route] per class, although this could be flexible.'

In practical lessons, such as a science lesson where pupils were measuring the length of shadows after constructing a model, there is often a rush to complete tasks and write up results. The nature of timed lessons often caused difficulty, and it was difficult for pupils to complete the work at home or at the start of another lesson. Teachers in their lesson planning often decided what tasks pupils needed to finish in lesson time and what exercises could be completed at another time. This was true of a Year 7 English lesson where pupils were asked to collaborate to compose a fairy tale, after discussing the nature of the characters generally found in these tales. Pupils were asked to finish the group task but were told that the individual writing task would be completed at another time. A geography teacher (who was also in charge of SEN) explained how she would make a point of seeing first those pupils who, she knew, would need extra time.

There were also examples of lessons where teachers introduced a common task and failed to provided any extension task when pupils finished early. One such lesson was seen with a Year 3 teacher who was responsible for teaching the middle range ability group. There was a general class introduction, with a session of questioning which lasted some three minutes. After this introduction the pupils were given two work sheets to complete. Two boys were kept under particular observation by the researcher. They were told to work together and finished the first worksheet after ten minutes. They were then required to look though a microscope to answer questions on the second sheet. This task was completed by both pupils after a further five minutes. This occurred ten minutes before end of lesson, when they were left to their own devices.

In one-third of the lessons which were observed, the majority of the pupils finished early, and were directed to other work, such as extra worksheets. In a number of secondary lessons there were also instances of pupils not finishing the tasks. In one Year 9 English lesson a common core task of devising a speech for one of the characters in Romeo and Juliet was expected to be covered at the same pace by all pupils; this resulted in over half the pupils not finishing it. In this case, the pupils were expected to provide an oral response which would it make it difficult for the class to return to this task again. More worryingly, there were some pupils who failed to complete written tasks in a number of different lessons, or were expected to do so as additional homework.

In their planning teachers devise tasks which are intended to suit the learning needs of their pupils and enable them to reach National Curriculum goals. If pupils are unable to benefit fully from such tasks because they cannot finish them off or have to rush them, then they are likely to lose motivation and fall further behind.

4.4 Reflecting on Classroom Practice

In this chapter we have reviewed what teachers believe are the priorities for classroom differentiation, how they plan their work to put these principles into action, and the way they respond to pupils' needs in the classroom. There were differences between the data on differentiation strategies obtained from lesson observation and from the survey, with observed practice failing to match the level of usage reported in the survey. There are a number of possible reasons for this, including the possibility that researchers saw an untypical sample of lessons. Nevertheless, the schools in the survey were a random sample, while the case-study schools had been selected because of their commitment to differentiation. Perhaps a more valid interpretation would be that even in such schools the scope of the challenge, in real classrooms, is daunting.

It is also important to stress the diversity of contexts we were observing. It should have become clear that the whole style and setting of primary classrooms provides a very different learning climate from most secondary subject lessons, for example, in scheduling, pace and social relationships, and these and other differences affect differentiation practice. It is particularly interesting, therefore, that in the survey secondary English teachers were the most likely of the three core subject groups to have similar principles and priorities to the primary teachers. But there were other dimensions of difference: in the character of the intake, in the pupil grouping framework and in the coherence of school policy and structures for differentiation – a topic we shall turn to in the next chapter. These differences undoubtedly affected what teachers did, in their planning and in their practice.

The most visible achievements, in both senses, were in what schools had done to plan for differentiation: that is, a great deal of work had been done to plan tasks and materials for varying levels of ability, to accommodate different learning styles and in some cases to define clear and explicit learning targets; and the evidence was there in the form of schemes of work, lesson outlines, resource banks and extension materials. The investment of time and professional expertise was very considerable and, in the best cases, incorporated the advice and contributions of learning support specialists. One primary school underlined the timescale, suggesting that it had taken five years to get all the Key Stage 2 teams to this stage, and most secondary schools recognised that departmental development was uneven. There was more chance of bringing all departments on board where there was clear pressure and support from senior managers.

In schools where this kind of investment was taking place, classroom teachers were in a stronger position, and in many cases had been closely involved in the development process – perhaps one of the best forms of professional development. But each teacher still had to translate plans into practice, and this is where it becomes much more difficult to feel confident about what is being achieved through differentiation strategies. Of course, there are many practical problems: too many pupils in each class, insufficient resources, not enough time for planning and review. But there are also more fundamental issues about delivering differentiation. Here two main concerns can be identified. First, many teachers may be working very hard at differentiation, but they are not working effectively enough, even within their own agreed principles. Secondly, and relatedly, most schools and teachers are only just developing a shared professional language in which to discuss achievement, among themselves and with their pupils. At this stage, we need to expand each of these points a little further.

There has been much discussion about whether policies are cost-effective. For our purposes, a more relevant idea is whether they are 'learning-effective'. That is, how effective are they at delivering learning, for every 'pound' of effort invested by the participants? This is the question we have tried to address and which has led us to query the effectiveness of some current investments in differentiation. The most obvious pointer relates to that key principle, 'knowing the pupils'. It was evident that efforts going into assessment of many kinds were not being put to sufficiently effective use in enabling teachers to 'know their pupils' and plan learning accordingly. A second indicator: only a minority of teaching teams, it seems, were putting as much effort into reviewing the impact of their materials as they did into materials development. Thirdly: were teachers sharing classroom expertise effectively, through whatever opportunities for shared teaching or structured observation could be created, so as to spread the best practice?

Lastly, and probably most importantly, were they being effective enough in enlisting pupils actively into the learning process? Most of the primary schools we visited were certainly working hard at developing pupils' abilities to manage the practical aspects of their work – finding resources, following instructions, working through a menu of activities. But there seemed to be some confusion about priorities. Was this mainly to free the teacher to spend more time with individuals? Because, if so, the risks, in time-wasting while pupils queued for help, or spun out their task, were considerable. Was it to offer 'choice' as one aspect of differentiation? If so, how could they avoid the hazards: pupils choosing the easy option, without sufficient challenge, or choice being restricted to the more able? In Key Stage 3, however, many of these issues did not even surface, since most pupils were not expected to exercise much autonomy or responsibility within their subject lessons; this was reserved for the completion of their out of school learning. Just when pupils' primary experience could have been usefully extended into a wider repertoire of skills to organise their learning and to set and reach targets, in too many instances they were expected to play a much more passive and conformist role. The 'cost' of this relative failure to enlist pupils fully in the learning process was to make the teacher's task, of knowing the pupils and meeting individual needs, proportionately harder.

The second issue concerns the development of a common language of achievement. We have seen that most teachers in the survey put 'responding flexibly' at the top of their list of practicable strategies. And yet, this proved quite difficult to discuss, with the teachers we interviewed, just because it was the everyday stuff of the (experienced) teacher: observing needs, directing appropriate questions, probing understanding, following up pupils' ideas. Some of these methods have been much discussed in teacher training, but they seldom seem to provide topics for discussion in staff meetings. Is this partly because there is not a readily used vocabulary, either for these strategies or for pupils' response? These are the kind of issues that were looked at in some detail in Postlethwaite's (1993) very useful review of differentiation in science, which considered the importance of diagnostic approaches linked with Assessment of Performance analyses. This issue is closely linked with the last one about pupil involvement, through the need for a language for sharing assessment criteria more readily with pupils, so that they begin to build a much more accurate and powerful understanding of what counts as success, rather than relying so heavily on grades and special incentives. The other way in which this development of a shared language could contribute to the first aim, of making practice more 'learning-effective', is by strengthening the value – already considerable – placed on LSAs and other support teachers. It was clear that in schools which had developed criteria and procedures for their LSAs to share professionally with teaching staff, more was being achieved to support a wider range of pupils.

5. DEVELOPING LEARNING: THE MANAGERS' ROLE

Senior and middle managers are uniquely placed to initiate change and to provide a supporting framework for differentiation at the classroom level. The impact which they felt their strategies had had and the factors influencing this will be explored in this chapter, as well as the role played by senior and middle managers in planning and supporting the differentiation process. The chapter will then go on to examine how senior managers in case-study and survey schools were preparing pupils (by organising class groups, monitoring progression and promoting pupil engagement in learning) and involving teachers (through professional support, development and appraisal) in their differentiation strategy.

5.1 The View from the Top

Can managers make a difference?

Senior managers were asked in the survey about the perceived impact that their differentiation strategies had had in enabling all Key Stage 2 or 3 pupils to maximise their achievements. Table 5.1 summarises their responses.

Table 5.1: Senior managers' perception of the impact of the school's differentiation strategy on pupils

Extent of Impact	Primary %	Secondary %
Considerable impact on most pupils	39	16
Considerable impact, in some years or subjects	24	32
Patchy impact – some pupils, subjects	19	35
Little impact – difficult to trace	14	15
No response	4	3
Total per cent	100	100
N =	405	292

Due to rounding errors, percentages may not always sum to 100.

The table shows a difference between the views of primary and secondary school leaders which was statistically and educationally significant. Almost two-thirds of primary headteachers considered that their differentiation strategy had had a 'considerable' impact on Key Stage 2 pupils, overall, or in some years or subjects; less than half the secondary managers felt this positive about the impact on Key Stage 3 pupils, and they were more likely to see the impact as 'patchy', and only related to some pupils in some subjects. Where either group identified the year groups or subjects where impact was most evident, it was the core subjects, particularly English and maths, that were most often mentioned.

Further (regression) analyses were undertaken to identify the factors associated with stronger perceived impact. These factors were derived from responses to other questions in the survey, particularly those asking about INSET and staff resources, about the way differentiation was integrated into whole-school planning and structures, and about the approaches which the school took to differentiation. In both phases, greater impact on pupils was associated with what schools saw as strong staff expertise and good whole-school support systems for differentiation (including coherent INSET and target-setting). In primary schools, a long-standing commitment to making differentiation a priority was also important. The ability of the intake did not emerge as a significant factor. However in secondary schools, those which were making differentiation a priority, because of overall pupil discipline and staffing pressures, were more likely to report impact on pupils. In other words, there seemed to be a strong incentive to make differentiation work in schools where the range of problems was most challenging.

Factors affecting the management of differentiation

In the case-study schools, we could explore more flexibly the factors they saw as important in helping them to implement their strategy effectively. Staff expertise was certainly seen as of crucial importance:

♦ The senior management at *Rock High* were aided by a staff who were committed and motivated to improving achievement at the school, and who endorsed the senior management's approach to solving this issue.

♦ *Cottage Primary,* with its very small team, had concentrated on developing their expertise as managers of learning, who could enhance pupils' own skills and responsibility.

Equally, senior managers identified the difficulty in bringing the whole staff on board:

♦ One secondary school, where there was a strong management lead on differentiation from the headteacher and some senior managers, had a number of teachers who had been at the school a long time and who were thought to be somewhat resistant to change.

♦ *Bankside High* school initially faced stiff opposition from staff members to the introduction of setting into the school, which had been committed to mixed ability. Staff felt that differentiation could, and indeed should be undertaken at the classroom level in mixed ability classes, and there was therefore a fundamental difference between the perceptions of staff and senior managers on what constituted a good management system to underpin differentiation.

Senior and middle managers in the survey schools were asked to rate some factors which they considered might promote or constrain an effective differentiation strategy in their particular school. These factors are shown in the box below.

1.	Time
2.	Staff motivation
3.	Staff expertise
4.	Resourcing
5.	In-class support
6.	Working groups/coordinators
7.	Classroom management
8.	Curriculum/timetable
9.	SEN support systems
10.	Class sizes
11.	Discipline

Figure 5.1 shows how senior managers rated these factors, which have been ranked according to the positive ratings given by primary heads. What the diagrams show is that most of these factors were seen as relevant to some extent. On the left can be seen the percentage of senior managers who considered the factor promoted effective differentiation in their school; on the right, the ratings showed where the factor was seen to be a constraint. (The space between the two bars indicates the proportion who saw the factor as irrelevant to an effective differentiation strategy.) Thus time (not enough of it!) was very widely seen as a constraint; less than ten per cent of the headteachers felt that time was on their side – that they had somehow managed to secure enough time for their staff to feel that this had helped them to implement their strategy. On the other hand, in both phases, the most important positive factor was the quality of the SEN support system: that is, they felt that having a good SEN support system promoted differentiation, and very few saw their SEN system as a constraint. In both these

instances, the factor was seen as important by over 90 per cent of the respondents. There were some factors that emerged as less critical – a substantial minority rated them as neither positive nor negative. Questions of discipline, having differentiation working groups or coordinators and curriculum/timetable considerations were not relevant factors for between 30 and 50 per cent of managers.

Figure 5.1 **Factors promoting or constraining effective differentiation in primary and secondary schools: senior managers**

Primary headteachers: factors influencing differentiation strategy

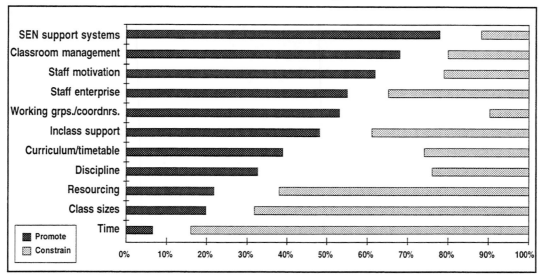

Secondary senior managers: factors influencing differentiation strategy

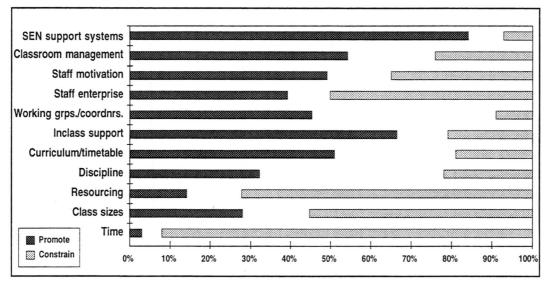

Based on 405 primary schools and 292 secondary schools.

From this evidence, it seems that, in the senior managers' view, good order, in the form of effective classroom management, together with support for those with special needs, were the most important preconditions for an effective differentiation strategy. There were, however, some differences between the two phases. In the primary schools, staff motivation and expertise were seen by over half the headteachers as important positive factors; secondary heads were more pessimistic, with more of them (50 per cent) seeing staff expertise as a constraint rather than a strength (39 per cent). For primaries, class size was (after time) the most significant constraint on effective differentiation.

The results of a similar analysis for secondary heads of department are shown in Figure 5.2. Heads of secondary English and maths, like their senior managers, stressed in-class support as a positive factor. Heads of all secondary subject departments also shared the primaries' concern about class size, with more of them seeing this as a constraint than did their senior managers. Among these core subject departments, the heads of maths took a rather more negative view than those of the other two subjects, with less than 60 per cent seeing any of these factors as promoting effective differentiation. Heads of science were the least likely to see staff motivation as relevant to their strategy.

Further analyses of this data showed there were underlying factors for each group. These were defined by the particular items which were most strongly associated with the factor. The data for each group of respondents was analysed separately, and the underlying factors which were identified for each group are shown below, with the main items defining them:

Staff capability (*Staff motivation and expertise*)	All groups
Individual support for pupils (*SEN system, in-class support*)	Heads of Department, Primary heads
Manageable classes (*Class sizes, discipline*)	Heads of Department
Resources (*Resourcing, time*)	Secondary senior managers

What the analysis shows is that these were identified as critical factors for an effective differentiation strategy. Direct comparisons could be made between the scores of the secondary heads of department on these underlying factors. These showed that English and maths leaders were significantly more likely than science colleagues to consider 'manageable classes' as a positive factor, promoting differentiation, and English teachers were more optimistic than science staff about staff capability. All three subjects identified the individual support factor as a positive influence.

Figure 5.2 Factors promoting or constraining effective differentiation in secondary schools: heads of department

Maths

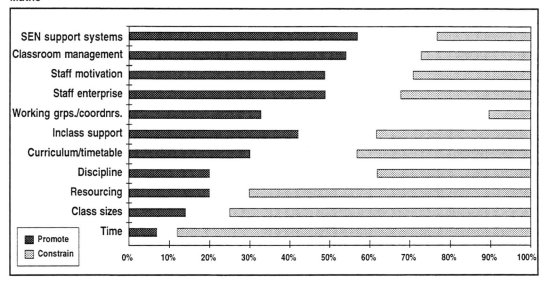

English

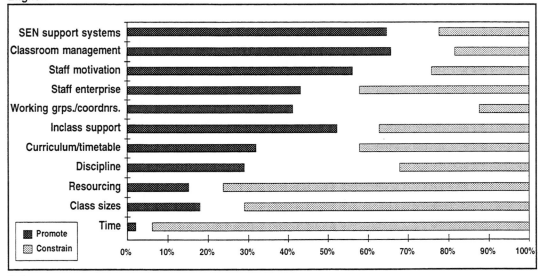

Science

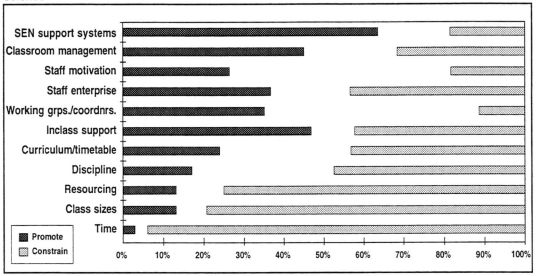

These findings suggest that there are clear patterns in what senior and middle managers consider is needed for effective differentiation, and they are closely concerned with classroom provision and staff capability. Compared with these, special measures such as working parties on differentiation are of little consequence. The concern about class sizes and time can be seen in part as a predictable response, but it also underlines the focus on support for individual learners, suggested by the stress on in-class support.

Another survey question explored these issues from a slightly different perspective, asking how relevant certain aspects of school life were to the development of an effective differentiation strategy. This question was asked of the primary heads and the secondary heads of department. For both groups, by far the most important item was 'knowing the pupils', with over 90 per cent of each group seeing this as 'wholly relevant' to an effective differentiation strategy, a point to which we will return later in this chapter. In other words, however it was to be achieved organisationally, almost all these experienced teachers considered that accurate and comprehensive information about each learner was wholly relevant to successful differentiation. It was a theme repeatedly stressed in the case-study schools, both by managers and classroom teachers. Not surprisingly, therefore, assessment was also seen as highly relevant, especially by primary teachers (over 80 per cent said it was wholly relevant). Interestingly, less than half of the survey respondents saw pupils' organisational skills as key, perhaps reflecting the impression coming from other evidence in the study that supported self study was rather seldom directly linked to differentiation practice.

Management style and priorities

How senior managers chose to implement their differentiation strategy depended partly on their overall leadership style and partly on the particular circumstances of the school, and the needs of the pupils and the staff. Having differentiation as a particular priority endorsed in some way by senior management was obviously also a motivating factor for teaching staff. In some of the case-study schools there was strong leadership from the top in dealing with differentiation, while in others the main impetus had either been devolved to middle managers or class teachers, or had originated with them.

♦ *Hillside High* was an example of a school with a strong commitment from the top to developing strategies for differentiation. A number of measures had been implemented relating to 'quality', such as Investors in People, defining strict targets in the SDP, and bringing in outside consultants to evaluate and advise on the way forward. An elaborate system of pupil grouping had also been put in place to address the low levels of achievement.

- At *Rock High*, the head was recognised as the 'driving force' behind differentiation, as in other aspects of school policy. However, the responsibility was shared with senior colleagues and the Learning Development Department had a key role in developing and maintaining structures that would promote differentiation. The senior and middle management played an important role, through support for curriculum development, by being committed to systematic monitoring and review through classroom observation, and by maintaining a caring, committed ethos throughout the school.

- *Lake High* ensured that differentiation had a high profile in the school by appointing a senior manager (not the headteacher) and a middle manager to have specific responsibility for differentiation. There were also a number of staff from different faculties who had a specified role in promoting and implementing differentiation. It was hoped that by appointing such a range of staff, the development of differentiation would be strengthened.

- *Abbey Primary* had a strong management figure in the headteacher, with a particular personal style which helped staff focus on differentiation as a priority. The senior management team sometimes went on weekend retreats to discuss policy moves and planning sessions. The head was committed to a complex organisational system, involving ability groups, subject-based carousels and team working within year groups. Indeed, team-working was felt to be very important in developing differentiation strategies, and this was promoted by senior management in the school at all levels of staff. However, the initiative for team-working had originally come from a group of staff.

- In contrast, *Windmill Primary* had a management style which was much more *laissez-faire*. The priority for this school was ensuring a calm, non-threatening ethos where the pupils could concentrate on learning. This was thought to be essential to a successful differentiation policy.

- The headteacher of *Cottage Primary* school had a more practical management style, probably due largely to her role as a full-time class teacher. There was no formal policy on differentiation at the school as such, but the whole school day was organised and choreographed to enable the small staff to spend as much time as possible in dealing with meeting the individual needs of all the pupils.

What comes across clearly from the case-study examples is that senior managers could and did differ in the importance they gave to differentiation within their overall school development strategy, and in the type of interventions they favoured. These might relate to structural or organisational matters: for example, pupil grouping, times for teacher planning, the place of differentiation in the School Development Plan. By contrast, in other schools the focus was much more strongly on improving learning approaches in the classroom, with senior managers looking for strategies to enhance teachers' professional skills.

In the survey, we tried to investigate more systematically the ways in which senior managers associated differentiation with other aspects of school life and development. We asked them how important it was as an aspect of certain other whole-school policies they might have. The answer, in general, was that for schools which had such policies (in practice, nearly all of them) differentiation was seen to be inextricably linked with most of them. Figure 5.3 shows the percentage of schools in each phase which saw differentiation as a very, or fairly, important aspect of the policies shown. In keeping with the evidence in the previous section, the most direct link was with policies on learning support, where three-quarters of the schools responding thought differentiation was a very important aspect of it. The main difference between the phases was in relation to assessment policy, where about three-quarters of primary heads, but only just over half their secondary colleagues, saw differentiation as integral to it. This finding supports other evidence from the survey and the case studies suggesting that primary staff were more likely to stress the need to base differentiation strategies on explicit evidence about individual pupil performance.

Figure 5.3   Perceived importance of differentiation as an aspect of whole-school policies

In primary schools

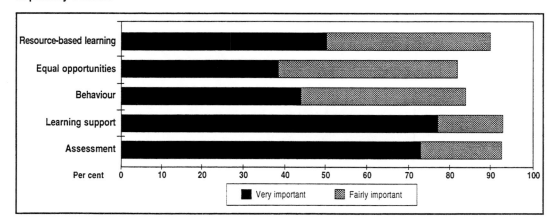

In secondary schools

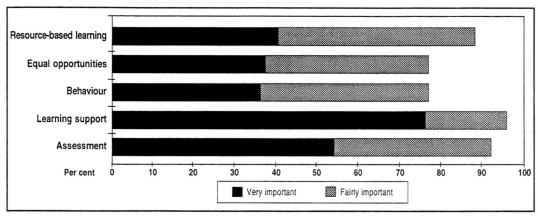

Differentiation and whole-school planning

Recognising that differentiation is indeed interwoven with other aspects of school planning, we wanted to know whether schools had a specific differentiation policy or strategy, or included differentiation as an aspect of other policies.

The secondary case-study schools were more likely than the primaries to have a policy specifically on differentiation. Some examples of those which did are given below:

♦   *Lake High* had an extensive written policy on differentiation, and one which most closely represented the public agenda. It highlighted four main types of differentiation; by task, by resource, by support and by response. Each of these four areas was discussed in the policy, and a named member of staff had responsibility for each one. Each type of differentiation was illustrated with its own diagram. A policy statement was also provided, which stated that, 'All students are unique individuals and need to find challenge and fulfilment in their work, and to be allowed to progress at the pace which is right for them.' The school had also recently developed a 'more able pupils' policy.

♦   *Hillside High* had a highly structured development planning system, with differentiation being explicitly included within departmental targets. In 1995/6, senior managers produced guidelines for heads of department to secure a 'moderated approach' to the preparation of departmental handbooks. These included the following questions on the policy for differentiation which was to form one element of the handbook:

  • Does it adequately cover and *support achievement* for the full ability range?

  • Is there a plan which acts as a model so that aspects, e.g. of a modular scheme of work, can be allocated to team members for completion?

  • Is there an overall plan where progress and progression, including remedial loops, are obvious?

  • Are pupils adequately targeted?

  • Are labels being inadvertently placed on pupils, e.g. resources offered, headings on worksheets?

  • Does the policy rely entirely on [sets] or is the overlap in ability at the borderlines recognised?

  • Is there a *diagrammatic* representation of the policy on differentiation to clarify a pupil's route through the scheme of work?

Departments can have been left in no doubt of the requirement to plan for differentiation; however, there was less guidance on what differentiation might look like in terms of classroom practice.

♦   At *Rock High*, there was a differentiation policy/action plan, which had been developed as part of the SDP some three years earlier, and was based on school practice. However, the policy was more fully and accurately reflected in a range of strategies at whole-school and departmental level. Differentiation policy in effect permeated procedures and priorities for appraisal (including classroom observation), INSET, curriculum development, pupil support, extra-curricular provision, parental involvement and governor programmes. Each department was expected to present its differentiation policy and there were also cross-curricular initiatives such as a spelling book for each pupil as part of a wealth of documentation on differentiation.

Primary schools were more likely to include differentiation within other documentation, but this might only appear in terms of general statements about meeting individual needs.

♦ *Lighthouse Primary* had as one of its current school development goals that they were to produce a policy on differentiation which would 'reflect actual school practice'.

♦ *Windmill Primary* had no differentiation policy, but differentiation was mentioned specifically in some subject policies.

In order to take account of the various ways in which differentiation policy might be expressed in whole-school planning documents, the survey asked senior managers to indicate which of a number of approaches they used. The results are summarised in Figure 5.4. For both phases, the most common approach was for schools to incorporate differentiation within other whole-school policy documents (about two-thirds said it was 'threaded through' the SDP), and to ensure that it was built into planning at subject level. Less than one-quarter of schools had a specific policy document on differentiation, although almost half the secondary senior managers reported that there was a specific section of their SDP devoted to it. The issue for schools was which approach was going to be more effective where it mattered, at classroom level. Here the key factors, in the case-study schools, were the extent to which policy statements were backed up by other aspects of planning – for example on staff development and appraisal – and the practical guidance on implementing differentiation that was available to teams of teachers.

Figure 5.4   Where and how differentiation policy is expressed in school documentation: primary and secondary schools

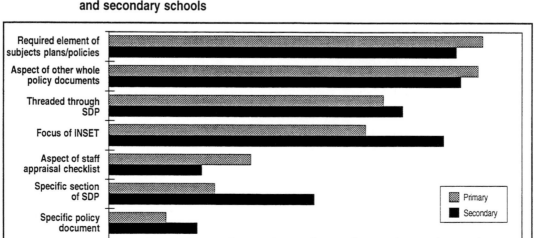

The survey provided an opportunity to investigate senior managers' perceptions of how they used all the levers available to them to develop and effective strategy. In other words, how did they translate their policy into practice? They were asked to indicate which of a number of strategies they used, and to assess how effective each was in implementing their policy. Figure 5.5 shows the proportion of schools using each strategy, and Figure 5.6 presents the perceived value of each to its users.

Figure 5.5   Strategies used by primary and secondary schools to implement differentiation

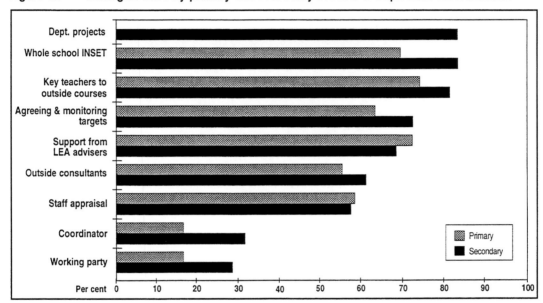

Secondary schools were significantly more likely than their primary counterparts to use many of these strategies – probably reflecting their size and the greater opportunity secondary schools have to deploy staff, whether on working parties or through INSET activities. This points up an underlying difference in style between the phases. In secondary schools, it was more usual to find activities and projects with a differentiation label, whereas in primary schools differentiation strategies, if they existed, tended to permeate 'everyday' practice. Indeed, in secondary schools, the departmental differentiation project was one of three most commonly used strategies. But less than one-third of schools in either phase allocated resources to staff time to co-ordinate differentiation programmes or serve on a working party. Interestingly, over half said they addressed differentiation through staff appraisal; as we shall see later (Section 5.3), this was not common practice in the case-study schools and the survey data does not tell us what actually took place.

Figure 5.6 has a different format. For each item, an 'effectiveness' score has been computed for those who used the strategy. The score runs from 0 (not very effective) to 2 (very effective). The first point to emerge is that, on average, few strategies were seen as more than 'fairly effective' (a score of 1). In general, primary schools were more likely than secondary schools to rate their differentiation strategies as effective. For each group, staff appraisal received the lowest score, suggesting that schools recognised that it was difficult to address differentiation practice in this way. Interestingly, those schools (primary or secondary) which had appointed a coordinator or a working party saw these as relatively effective strategies. Secondary schools were, not surprisingly, most positive about their generally preferred strategy of departmental differentiation projects.

Figure 5.6 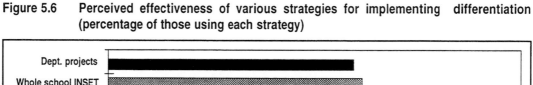 Perceived effectiveness of various strategies for implementing differentiation (percentage of those using each strategy)

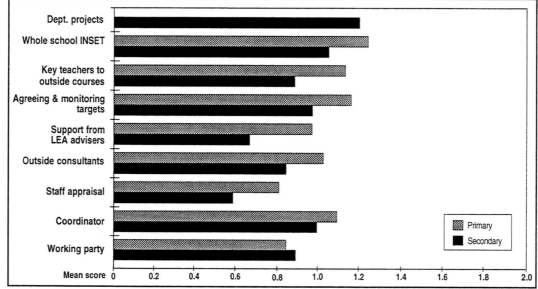

One of the important consequences of this departmental approach was the uneven pace of development, and the challenge this presented to senior managers. Many of the case-study secondary schools were moving towards differentiation at different rates across the departments, but there were some who had managed to bring the good work of individual departments together into a coherent and effective whole-school strategy.

◆ At *Bankside High* individual departments were still initiating strategies for differentiation, which the senior management were then endeavouring to promote throughout the school. A researcher from a nearby university was asked into the school to compile a report on staff attitudes to the global introduction of setting, as a strategy for differentiation. This revealed much negativity among staff which had impeded progress towards a whole-school strategy for differentiation.

◆ *Hillside High* had also battled against the uneven motivation of staff in implementing senior management-led strategies for differentiation. While English, maths and science departments had responded actively and creatively, developing their own (rather different) agendas, some other departments were more reluctant. Alongside these departmental initiatives, progress was still being made in the whole school initiatives for individual target setting and monitoring of pupils' progress, as well as setting.

♦ *Rock High* had made tremendous progress over the previous eight years of concerted effort in promoting differentiation in the school. Particularly effective had been the classroom monitoring and paired teaching, for reviewing and disseminating good practice. Nevertheless, departmental progress had been uneven, with some departments waiting for a change of leadership before real change took place. Staff commitment and motivation were seen to be crucial in the success of the various strategies implemented.

Some of the evidence gathered in case-study schools has suggested that, although much may be happening in a school at the management level, translating this into good teaching practice in the classroom is a more problematic undertaking. It is therefore crucial that the management approach to the teaching staff is coherent and well thought out. As we saw at the beginning of this chapter, headteachers themselves recognised the central importance of staff expertise for a successful differentiation strategy.

Two aspects of managing practice are the level of staff consultation, and the extent to which staff feel they have involvement and ownership. Most of the case-study secondary schools reported regular consultation and information-sharing between senior and middle managers, and there was an assumption of a trickle-down effect through departmental meetings. In all but the largest primary schools, communication and consultation were both more informal and generally more inclusive, since they often involved all the staff. However, the head of *Abbey Primary,* with a staff of 23 full-time teachers, three nursery nurses and 12 welfare assistants, had to develop more formal consultation procedures. For the purposes of addressing differentiation issues, probably the most important (in addition to the SMT planning meetings) were the regular team sessions, for the three teachers in each year group, and the whole-staff meetings or INSET sessions, which sometimes took the form of weekend residentials or 'away days'.

The broader issues of staff involvement and management of differentiation will be considered in 5.3, after we have returned to the largest and most central constituency: the pupils. Although the working out of differentiation takes place in the classroom, senior managers have the scope for strongly influencing the classroom context and the learning skills which pupils bring to it.

5.2 Managing Pupils

Senior and middle managers have two main options for managing pupils in ways which may facilitate differentiation: organisationally, by controlling the composition of teaching groups and much more broadly, through a whole range of measures designed to enhance the responsibility which pupils themselves take for their learning. We shall look first at the use of pupil grouping strategies.

Grouping strategies

The survey and the case studies both suggest that, although many teachers were reluctant to say that differentiation was 'mainly' about ability grouping, many schools have reported an increase in the proportion of pupils taught for at least some of the time in classes grouped by ability; and this shift has coincided with the period when differentiation has become a higher priority. Perhaps surprisingly, primary heads were more likely than their secondary colleagues to associate differentiation with 'grouping "like" pupils together'. Our case-study evidence suggested that this contrast reflected real differences in practice, with primary teachers grouping pupils by ability for specific purposes *within* a mixed ability class group, while secondary managers applied the statement to more formal setting or streaming arrangements, and only one fifth of them thought this was what differentiation was mainly about.

The survey results pointed to an increase in ability grouping or setting, in both primary and secondary schools over the last three years (Figure 5.7).

Figure 5.7:   Use of setting, as reported for 1992/3 and 1995/6: percentage of schools where setting (rather than mixed ability) predominated in Key Stage 2 and Key Stage 3

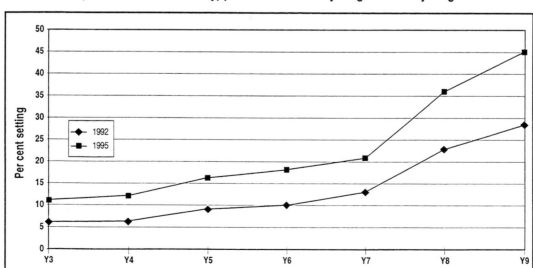

Based on responses from responses from 284 primary schools and 292 secondary schools.

Figure 5.7 shows two trends: the increase in setting by age, particularly in the secondary school (Year 7 and 9); and the perceived change in policy over time. As these school managers saw it, the trend was for more ability grouping in each age group of Key Stage 2 and 3, although the 1992-5 increase had been steepest for Year 9, perhaps reflecting pressure to prepare for stratified GCSE papers in Year 10 and 11. Nevertheless, the increase should not be overstated; only just over half these primary schools reported any setting for Key Stage 2 in 1995, with about one-third introducing it for one or two subject areas, usually maths and/or English. Moreover, there was little increase in setting in these subjects from Year 3 to Year 6. Figure 5.8 shows the number of subjects in which there was setting for each of these year groups, illustrating the very gradual increase. It seemed as if schools decided on a policy for Key Stage 2 and applied it, with only minor changes, to all year groups.

Figure 5.8   Setting in Key Stage 2

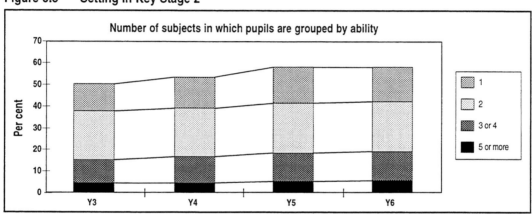

In Key Stage 3, by contrast, there was a steep incline, with setting increasing in most subjects from Year 7 to Year 9 (Figure 5.9).

Figure 5.9   Percentage of secondary schools setting in Key Stage 3 on basis of subject attainment

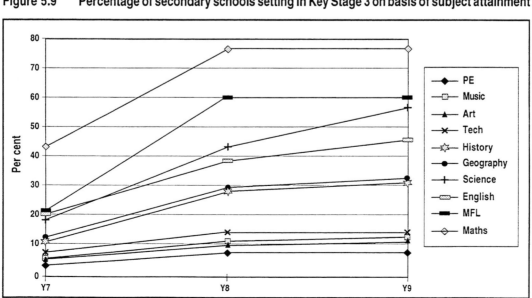

The graph shows the clear and predictable hierarchy of subjects in each year, with setting most common in maths and foreign languages. In these subjects, a plateau had been reached by Year 8, by which time 60 per cent of schools were setting by attainment in languages and 75 per cent in maths. In science, the proportion of schools setting by attainment continued to increase through Key Stage 3, from less than 20 per cent in Year 7 to 56 per cent in Year 9. Perhaps more surprisingly, English followed a rather similar, if less steep, increase, with nearly half the schools (45 per cent) setting by Year 9. It seems that by 1995/96, setting was becoming established as a common, though not universal, pattern for the core subjects. Just under one-fifth of the secondary schools banded or streamed their Year 7 tutor groups. It is therefore likely that the proportion of pupils in ability-based class groups of some kind is rather greater than Figure 5.9 suggests.

Figure 5.10 deals with a related issue: the information which schools used in forming groups. The decision to group classes according to ability, and the information on which the grouping was based, differed for Key Stage 2 and Key Stage 3, reflecting the different organisational approach in each phase. In primary schools, only just over one-third of the schools used assessment information to form class groups in Year 3. Of course, many schools would not have more than one Year 3 class, and as we have seen, could use some form of setting within the class. By contrast, three-quarters of the secondary schools used assessment data in forming their Year 7 groups, but the main reason for doing so was to ensure that each group represented the full ability range.

Figure 5.10: Types of information used to form class groups

Primary (Year 3)

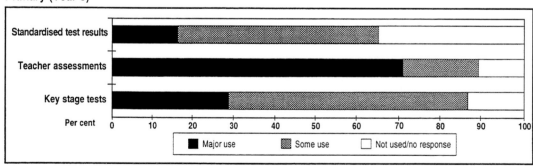

Secondary (Year 7)

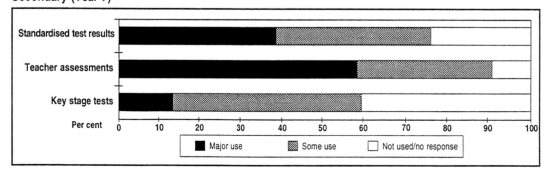

For both sets of managers, teacher assessments were the main source of information, but secondary schools were more likely to use standardised tests for forming groups. They were even less likely than primary schools to use key stage test results for this purpose.

How far was the decision to opt for ability grouping, either in the form of banded classes or through setting, an explicit strand of differentiation, and who took the decision? To address this issue we need to turn to the case-study evidence.

In all the case-study schools, senior and middle managers had structured pupil teaching groups in some way related to their differentiation policy, usually on a departmental, or year-group basis. One or two of the case-study schools had deliberately developed formal ability-based grouping as a key plank of their differentiation strategy. For example, in *Hillside High*, with a nine-form entry intake skewed towards the lower end of the ability range, ability banding was seen as a necessary first step, to make it easier for teachers to develop and implement effective differentiation classroom strategies.

♦ The senior management team had decided to create bands or Narrow Ability Groups (NAGs). The entry group was divided into two parallel halves (in terms of ability (all Year 6 pupils in the LEA took the AH3 reasoning test) and each of these halves was then divided into three ability bands (A, B and C) with a remedial band (F). The F classes, identified by the head of SEN before entry, had a higher teacher-pupil ratio and a separate timetable for part of the week. The C classes (covering about 46 pupils with low literacy scores) had two teachers each for core subjects. In this way, the head felt, the common curriculum could be tailored to group level. Logistics prevented setting by subject, so he recognised that the A/B banding might not suit all subjects.

In practice, subject departments in the school differed in the way they planned their work across the bands, and each department was required to set out their specific differentiation strategies and targets in line with the SDP.

♦ The science department, for example, who had been rewriting their Key Stage 3 course in modular form, used the NAG structure to align the scheme of work, with its built-in differentiation. Thus, F groups were not expected to go beyond Level 4, C groups up to Level 5, B groups to Level 6, and A groups up to Level 7. But these guidelines were flexible in enabling individuals to progress appropriately, since the materials for all levels were available within modules. The head of science saw the grouping structure as necessary, but not sufficient, for differentiation; it provided a framework within which to develop their own approach.

One large primary school, *Abbey Primary,* had also, unusually among the case-study primaries, opted for a whole-school setting structure for Key Stage 2, based on performance in maths, English and humanities:

♦ The school had a complex system of grouping pupils, which relied on fairly extensive assessment information based on National Curriculum requirements. At the start of Year 3 there was a diagnostic period of four weeks, and then three groupings were made according to ability in maths, humanities and English across the year group. The lower band in each year-group was 'stepped', so that there was a group for children with special educational needs. In Year 6, even finer grouping was being introduced, so that three ability groups were defined within each class group. A carousel system was also in operation which allowed children access to specialist teaching once a fortnight.

One secondary SMT, at *Lake High*, had deliberately devolved decisions about pupil grouping to middle managers. A block timetabling approach had been adopted to encourage departments to devise pupil grouping systems that would be appropriate to their teaching approach. The science department had used the block timetabling system to develop flexible grouping procedures. Interestingly, one of the factors which they felt had facilitated this approach was that they had a stable staff in the department, who were used to working together, and had in fact worked this strategy out together. Staff supplied further details of the procedure.

♦ The flexible grouping procedure was used to remove groups of students from the mainstream at various points in the curriculum, and for different reasons. Sometimes a top group was selected to get more intensive teaching from a specialist teacher. Sometimes the lower achievers across the year group were brought together for revision of the basic lesson. Because these were *ad hoc* and interchangeable groupings, they believed there was less stigma attached, and because of the flexible nature of groupings, students could move in and out of the groups for different topics. The decision to move students was dependent on a thorough diagnostic testing system, based on three levels of ability.

At *Rock High* the head had tackled the rather confused practice on grouping systematically, developing a general policy over several years. This was set out in a policy statement on 'Pupil groupings within subjects':

♦ We are not a setting school or a mixed ability school but will group pupils according to how we believe they will best learn. Our priority is to maximise the achievement of each individual and, in so doing, to raise pupil achievement across the school. The guidance for achieving this situation is as set out below.

♦ Each department must agree with the Senior Management Team a coherent plan for pupil grouping which covers all five year groups. The plan *must* include a written rationale and be included in each department's handbook. The rationale should include reasons for decisions and how the choice of grouping will maximise pupil learning.

♦ Pupil groupings should take into consideration staff expertise, resources, National Curriculum requirements and past exam results.

The policy document went on to list criteria which departments must use in placing pupils in sets, or moving them: sets were to be reviewed each half term. The outcome was in line with national trends, with an increase in setting from Year 8. Maths and modern languages departments set during Year 7, humanities and science from Year 8. Only English and technology departments kept pupils in mixed ability groups throughout Key Stage 3. More interesting is the process by which they had arrived at their existing practice. This had involved detailed discussions between the head of department and the SMT, bearing in mind resources and staffing.

The whole topic of pupil grouping has of course been the subject of major studies over the years (Alexander, Rose and Woodhead, 1992; GB. OFSTED, 1993) and cannot be done full justice here. However, it has been given new force by the recent White Paper, *Excellence in Schools* (GB. P. HofC, 1997) which 'makes the presumption that setting should be the norm in secondary schools' and that 'in some cases, it is worth considering in primary schools'. In the White Paper, it is clearly explained that the rationale for this is 'to ensure that all children, whatever their talents, develop their diverse abilities'. The trends identified in the survey would suggest that schools have largely anticipated these recommendations. Our case-study evidence, however, suggests that how and why pupil grouping arrangements are made and implemented will continue to be as important as – perhaps even more important than – the arrangements themselves. How are in-class ability groups formed in primary classes? What do pupils make of these early experiences of being identified within an 'ability' hierarchy? Is it largely an organisational device (to allocate different tasks or resources), or is work arranged so that pupils learn from each other, within and across these groups? How do all pupils benefit from arrangements to satisfy the twin goals of specialist teaching and setting by ability? In secondary schools, how much investment, in Year 7, goes into discussing and pursuing individual progression, from Year 6 achievements through the Year 7 curriculum, compared with entry testing and set-forming? Are procedures to move pupils between sets really as flexible as the senior management team would intend? And what about other approaches to pupil grouping, for shorter periods, or across age groups?

For the purposes of this study, the main interest in pupil grouping arrangements was to evaluate their function within the school's overall differentiation strategy. It was clear that solutions depended partly on context and partly on educational philosophy, but that there was a an emerging common purpose: to adopt solutions that facilitated the goal of raising attainment. What seemed to be needed was clear thinking leading to agreed criteria for decisions on grouping, which would be in line with this goal, avoiding the well-known dangers of negative labelling for lower ability groups. Schools which had thought seriously about differentiation were also aware that any grouping arrangements came under the 'necessary but not sufficient' heading; they might simplify the teacher's task, but differentiation remained a pedagogical challenge which could not be 'solved' by these procedural decisions.
Systems for managing pupil assessment

We have seen that senior managers themselves, as well as their staff, put 'knowing the pupils' at the top of their agenda, as a basis for effective differentiation. This was the only factor which received a stronger endorsement than assessment in its relevance to developing an effective strategy for differentiation – over 90 of per cent of each group considering it 'wholly' relevant. Since the aim of assessment could be seen as to 'know the pupils' as learners, this strengthens the importance of assessment, formal and informal, as a key component of the support system for effective differentiation. Figure 5.11 shows in full the responses of primary heads and secondary heads of department on the relevance of assessment to their differentiation strategy.

Almost all the respondents saw assessment as at least 'partly' relevant to differentiation. Heads of science were the least likely to judge it 'wholly' relevant, but in fact over almost two-thirds did so. So here was a clear acknowledgement of the association by a wide range of managers. What can managers do to ensure that teachers' knowledge of pupils and their progress in learning is actually shared between teachers, so that time is not wasted rediscovering pupils' strengths and weaknesses? While this seems particularly important at pupil transition points of any kind – end of year, change of school – it is also a cross-curricular challenge, if more than one teacher is involved with a pupil or group. This challenge, only too familiar in secondary schools, is now facing Key Stage 2 teachers in primary schools which have introduced some specialist teaching for older classes.

Figure 5.11: Relevance of assessment in developing an effective differentiation strategy

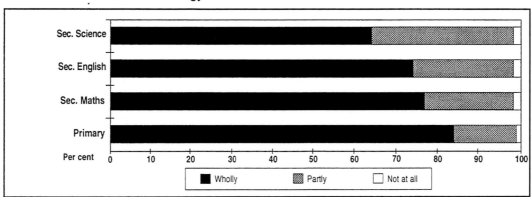

Evidence from the case-study schools suggested that, although managers were aware of the need to create common and transparent assessment systems, which could provide diagnostic feedback in the classroom, it was extremely difficult to convince all the staff, especially subject colleagues in secondary schools, of the pedagogical advantages of a common assessment system.

We have seen that classroom-based diagnostic use of assessment was uncommon in most of the subject areas we investigated in case-study schools. Similarly, the survey suggested that only in English were more than one-third of core subject secondary teachers claiming to use assessments to plan individual targets within their own lessons. In Key Stage 2 lessons, however, almost half the teachers claimed to do so, suggesting that the principle of exploiting assessment data for improving teaching was well understood, however hard it might be to realise. At best, common assessment systems could create a shared and therefore 'transparent' language for monitoring individual progress. More often, different groupings (year or subject teams) had developed their own assessment procedures, tools and 'language', even where there was a nominally common framework. Indeed, in many cases, systems for recording pupil attainment seemed to be angled more towards reporting and accountability (to parents, system) rather than to professional communication and sharing knowledge on pupils' attainment across subjects and year groups. However, there were examples of whole-school or departmental strategies to apply assessments diagnostically, to feed back into learning.

♦ In *Rock High* there was evidence of assessment evidence being used diagnostically with pupils through a system of one-to-one targeting sessions with each child at least once a term.

♦ In *Hillside High* attempts were also made to use assessment diagnostically through their Integrated Curriculum Assessment system (ICA), a type of individual review based on cross-curricular assessments.

127

♦ In *Cottage Primary*, there were ongoing diagnostic assessments, with Friday afternoons being set aside to review progress and targets with individual pupils, while the rest of the class were engaged in non-National Curriculum activities.

♦ In *Lake High,* diagnostic assessment was used in the Science department to inform decisions about moving students from group to group, depending on their performance in different modules of work.

The other, related option for managing information on pupil performance is to devise some form of individual tracking and feedback system. In the case-study schools, this kind of tracking system was often confined to those most 'at risk'.

♦ One whole-school example of a system of this kind was at *Lake High*, where they had set up a tracking system through the Learning Advice Department. Students who had been identified from various sources as having some kind of need, whether it be learning support or behavioural difficulties, were placed on the tracking system on a termly rota, and the policy required each identified child to see a teacher at least once a term. There were logistical problems, however. Teachers were selected for this task because they had some time available rather than because of their expertise or commitment; as a result, staff motivation was not high, and this had had an unfortunate effect on the perceived value and success of this system.

By 1995 several of the secondary schools were introducing the kind of mentoring systems which have become common in the last few years, to track and support certain 'at risk' pupils. At *Rock High*, in 1994-5 there were two Year 11 groups, labelled 'Operation Boost' (for those with predicted A-C grades) and 'Operation Salvage' for those likely to get lower grades. Pupils were identified for the mentoring scheme using a variety of test scores and in-school assessments, with mentors being mainly heads of department. But the school recognised this was only addressing the needs of a small minority. Since 1995, other work on target-setting (GB. OFSTED, 1996; see also Schagen and Weston, *et al.*) has shown how such schemes can be refined and extended, to more age groups and a higher proportion of pupils.

At least one school was already involved in a value-added project through their LEA, and was beginning to explore how the findings could be used to evaluate pupils' progress, and also the relative effectiveness of learning within different subjects. The evidence from this study, however, suggested that there was much to be done if all the effort that went into assessment procedures was to be effectively harnessed to improve teaching and learning. There seemed to be several major components, all of which were needed.

1. **Develop agreed standards and assessment 'language' within subjects.** This was clearly developing through moderation procedures within and between schools.

2. **Develop agreed criteria and a common 'language' across subjects.** This seemed to be a much greater challenge, with a tension between encouraging autonomy and securing common standards.

3. **Ensure that recording systems can be and are used for professional evaluation as well as reporting.** Do staff really use assessments to evaluate their teaching and to plan learning for individuals and groups?

4. **Make assessment data on individuals across the curriculum readily available to all staff.** This has always been a major challenge for secondary schools, and many systems have proved unwieldy. Without such information, pupils' achievements and problems in a range of skills needed for many subjects may be ignored.

5. **Build assessment-related targets into schemes of work.** Too often, assessment was still being treated, in topics, unit and modules, only as an outcome activity, rather than a starting point for learning targets.

6. **Involve pupils in the process!** As we saw in Chapter 3, pupils were fairly accurate self-assessors, but were not often encouraged to take an active part in assessment. As one teacher put it, self-assessment is also about empowerment and confidence, since many pupils have low expectations of themselves.

The transformation that seemed to be needed was to apply the very considerable knowledge that a school has about its pupils' achievement to the effective planning of learning, rather than restricting it largely to the reporting and analysis of outcomes. Perhaps one of the most productive avenues is the last in the list above, the active involvement of pupils, and it is to this whole issue of strategies for developing the pupils' role in the learning process that we now turn.

Systems for developing pupils' self-management

In Chapter 3 we have seen how pupils themselves talked about the strategies they used to manage their work, whether or not this was actively encouraged by the school. Indeed in the case studies it was easier to identify initiatives to encourage a degree of pupil autonomy in primary than in secondary schools. For example:

♦ *Lighthouse Primary* had used resourcing to encourage a measure of pupil responsibility, by organising the resource areas identically across the school. Children then had the confidence to access the resources they felt they needed as and when they wished, having gained the teacher's permission. The school had also experimented recently with mixed age classes due to recent cuts, and increases in pupil numbers. This was considered to have been a success. Older pupils teamed up with younger ones, and this was felt to give them more self-esteem and a feeling of responsibility, which might benefit them as self-managers.

♦ *Windmill Primary* school promoted the idea of pupils as self-managers, by trying to create an atmosphere in which pupils could fulfil their potential and feel relaxed and safe. *Bankside High* was also involved in developing an effective school ethos.

♦ *Cottage Primary* probably had the most explicit example of positive strategies towards developing pupils as self-managers. Each individual child had their own timetable, which they followed throughout the day. They were able to work quietly and independently on this, which left the teacher free to concentrate on individual groups on a rotational basis. The system began in Key Stage 1 and drew on the findings of the 'High Scope' programme (Schweinhart and Weikart, 1997).

♦ *Observatory Primary* promoted the idea of pupils being self-managers through the laptop project, which enabled each child to be working at their own pace on the laptop, and developing skills of manipulation and tutelage (towards both other children and teachers), which was thought to result in improved self-esteem and an improvement in the quality of the work they were able to produce on their own.

On the other hand, we noted in Chapter 4 that there were difficulties with the concept of pupil autonomy. First, pupils had to be carefully taught the skills they needed to manage their work, to collaborate with others, to plan their use of time. Secondly, autonomy and choice could, in the hands of less experienced teachers, slide into poor use of time and lack of challenge. As schools in both phases were appreciating, the only effective route to independent learning was through a carefully graded programme of skill-building and the structured offer of appropriate choices. There were examples of this process at work in some of the case-study schools, but it was not yet a fully developed strategy, at senior management level, in any of them. It was easier to see the process at work, at secondary level, outside the timetable; for example, in opportunities for extension work after school or on Saturdays. None of these schools had adopted systematic programmes to teach 'thinking skills' or other forms of cognitive training such as concept mapping, intended to equip pupils with tools to boost their learning in any area of the curriculum. Development was more likely to occur through the Record of Achievement process of individual review or some other form of profiling. The challenge here was to integrate tutorial and subject specialist initiatives.

As we shall see in the final chapter, which includes an update on developments in the case-study schools, several of them are already adopting the language and mechanisms relating to individual target-setting, with its underlying assumption of greater pupil participation in, and responsibility for the management of learning. In order to develop this process, senior managers are likely to find themselves under greater pressure to take the initiative, since the process of involving pupils in this way may well present a major culture change for many teachers.

5.3   Teachers as Managers of Differentiation

Most senior managers accepted that it was one of their key responsibilities to create appropriate staffing structures to implement their differentiation policy and to develop and support teacher expertise. How did they use these powers? We shall look at two main topics: the allocation of responsibilities, with particular emphasis on the role of middle managers and of the SENCO; and professional development and review.

Allocating responsibilities for differentiation

In the survey, schools were asked whether there was a named person who was responsible for differentiation and, if so, what other role they held. Only 20 per cent of primary schools had identified it as an explicit responsibility, but over two-thirds of secondary schools had done so. For the primaries who had taken this step, the most likely postholder to be identified as responsible for differentiation was the SENCO. In secondaries, the picture was more complex.

Table 5.2   Responsibility for differentiation in primary and secondary schools

	Secondary %	Primary %
Senior management team	39	NA
Departments/subjects	43	3
SENCO	18	11
In other roles	9	3
All staff	4	1
None specified	31	80
N =	292	405

In the secondary survey since more than one response could be given, percentages do not sum to 100.

The question was asked in a different format in each phase. Respondents were asked whether the first two groups identified in Table 5.2 had some specific responsibility. In almost 40 per cent of schools, senior managers and heads of subject departments were involved. Less than one-fifth identified the SENCO as being responsible for differentiation, despite their key role in implementing differentiation policy.

Although few primaries specified 'all staff', they may well have implied this by not identifying a specific postholder; or in practice the differentiation strategy was one of the head's responsibilities. Where the heads in case-study primaries had allocated oversight of the strategy to the SENCO or another member of staff, this was defined in rather general terms, such as the preparation of guidelines or the monitoring of classroom practice. In most of the secondary schools the SMT's responsibility was shared with middle managers, with heads of department playing an important role. It was they who worked out how to turn general guidelines into classroom practice, and here we need to look at the survey and case-study evidence on their strategic approach, for their own departments and for the school as a whole, relating it to the accounts in Chapter 4 of how they worked with their teams in planning for differentiation.

The role of middle managers. The heads of the maths, science and English departments were asked in the survey about the management of their own departments in terms of differentiation. In Figure 5.12, the total length of the bar shows the proportion of the heads of department who said they had a written departmental policy on learning approaches; the hatched section of the bar indicates the percentage who indicated that their policy specifically addressed differentiation.

Figure 5.12   Percentage of secondary subject departments having a learning policy which addresses differentiation

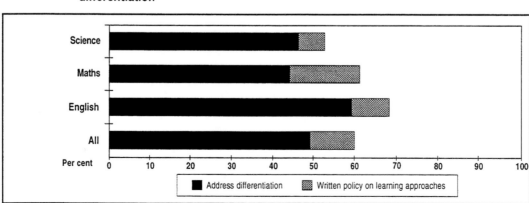

Based on all heads of department responding to the survey (559).

The responses showed significant differences between the subjects. Heads of English were most likely to have a written policy and, overall, they were the group most likely to address differentiation. But if a science department had a written policy, it was actually more likely than policies for the other subjects to tackle differentiation. This fits with other evidence in the survey and the case studies to suggest that, although general awareness of differentiation seemed to be higher among English teachers than in other subjects, those science departments which were interested and concerned about teaching and learning methods had built differentiation into their review.

There was much less difference between the subject departments on another key issue: the amount of practical support they received, from within or beyond the school, for improving differentiation in their classes. The survey responses are given in Figure 5.13.

Figure 5.13   Practical support for differentiation: views of secondary heads of department

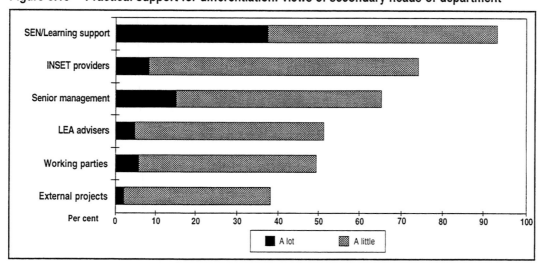

The heads of department clearly valued their Learning Support colleagues above all other groups, in terms of practical support. They were the only group felt by more than a quarter of the respondents to give 'a lot' of help. Here there was a significant difference between the subjects, again with English staff the most likely to value support from Learning Support – almost half thought they received 'a lot' of help, compared with 30 per cent of science staff and 35 per cent of maths staff. Although the majority of heads of department acknowledged 'a little' support from other sources, it did not seem to have much impact. In general, these results are in line with the views of these heads of department, presented at the start of the chapter, on the factors which they felt were important for an effective differentiation strategy (Figure 5.2).

Perhaps of most concern, from Figure 5.13, was one other factor not included in the earlier list: less than one-fifth thought their senior management team provided 'a lot' of practical help. This suggests a lack of confidence in the Senior Management Team's capacity to provide effective support and leadership for the central task of achieving effective learning for all pupils. It could be that the response is partly explained by the stress in the question on 'practical support', since heads of department would hardly expect senior managers to provide hands-on help in the classroom. But there are many other appropriate forms of practical support that would be relevant, in the form of funds for materials, equipment or additional support staff, staff development and training, or better links with the learning support staff.

These results raise several issues. First, the much-appreciated help from learning support colleagues was not apparently seen as part of an overall strategy for more effective learning led by senior managers. Second, they imply some scepticism about the amount of 'practical' help on offer from senior managers. Lastly, these heads of department did not see 'a lot' of practical support coming from any external source. It appeared that, in the view of the majority, differentiation was a challenge which depended primarily on them and their subject team, with some help from SEN specialists, rather than a concerted whole-school programme to which they contributed.

In the case-study primary schools, where differentiation policy was generally led by the head teacher, middle managers also had a key planning role in some instances:

♦ In *Windmill Primary* and *Lighthouse Primary*, the subject coordinators had a role in planning topic work throughout the school in three levels of ability.

♦ In *Abbey Primary*, middle managers had been responsible for creating the organisational framework, which grouped pupils of similar levels of ability together. Lesson planning teams throughout the school were co-ordinated by middle management.

The secondary schools provided a number of interesting examples of a more generic role played by middle managers in the differentiation process.

♦ At *Lake High*, in addition to there being a named person responsible for differentiation at the senior management level, there was also one at the middle management level, who liaised with the different faculties in trying to maintain differentiation at the forefront of the priority list. Members of the faculties got together in a differentiation development group, which met once a term to review progress. All the faculties had differentiation as a current priority in their action plans. Despite this level of staffing commitment to differentiation, it was felt by this particular coordinator that differentiation was not as high a priority this year, as it had been in previous years, and the main challenge for this year was in creating a common terminology. Interestingly, the senior manager in charge of differentiation felt that the main priority this year was putting all the theory about differentiation into practice.

♦ At *Rock High*, the middle managers had a much more practical role. They covered lessons to enable class teachers to observe one another's lessons, as a tool for monitoring, moderating and disseminating good practice in differentiation. This had been going on for a number of years, and was found to be extremely useful in promoting differentiated teaching and learning practices. Middle managers at times went into classrooms themselves to monitor practice, and they were felt to be less threatening to teaching staff than senior managers. (At these times, senior managers would go in and cover for the middle managers.) They were also regularly brought together in progress and development meetings with other faculty heads to discuss any issues that were arising. In this school, middle managers had an integral part in the monitoring and evaluation of differentiation and in the process of disseminating good practice across the school.

In this school and at *River High,* heads of department were working within a framework supported and led by the SEN specialists who had been given this role as part of the whole-school strategy. This opens up new possibilities which we review below.

The role of the SENCO in managing differentiation

As we saw in Chapter 2, much of the drive to develop and implement differentiation within the classroom, in the form of more appropriate pedagogy targeted at learning needs, has come from specialists trained as SEN specialists and working collaboratively with subject specialists. In recent years, it has been widely recognised that they have a responsibility not only for those with specific learning difficulties or disabilities and also for those with exceptional gifts, but for helping teachers to meet the learning needs of all pupils. However, since the introduction of the Code of Practice following the 1993 Education Act (GB. Statutes, 1993), SEN Coordinators, (SENCOs) have taken on very specific responsibilities related to the identification of special educational needs, in keeping with the requirements of the Code of Practice (GB. DfEE, 1994). The SENCO's role description includes responsibility for supporting other staff, through advice and in-service training, thus re-reinforcing the advisory function which has developed in many schools. But in practice, especially in primary schools where the SENCO was often also a class teacher, identifying individual needs and liaising with external agencies could greatly reduce the time for this wider support role. For this reason, we wanted to know, from the national survey, how far senior managers felt their SENCOs and any other staff with SEN responsibilities, could contribute actively to their overall differentiation strategy.

Figure 5.14 shows their responses to a question about the support offered to other staff.

Figure 5.14   Ways in which SENCO/SEN staff support other teachers: primary and secondary schools

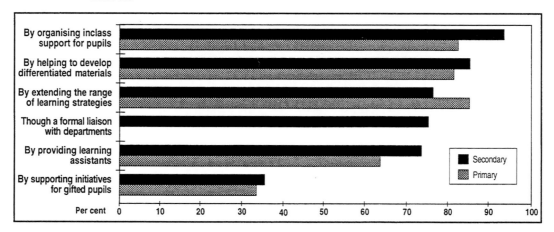

As the figure suggests, there were differences between primary and secondary schools in the relevance they accorded to these five strategies. Here they have been ranked according to the priorities allocated by secondary schools. For both phases, the SEN role in providing direct, in-class support for individuals was very important, but it was significantly more important in secondary schools. In part, this may indicate the greater resources available to secondaries who were also more likely to value the provision of learning assistants. Three-quarters of the secondary schools had created a formal structure for ensuring SEN staff could work with departments – again, reflecting the more complex systems needed in secondary schools. For primaries, it was the SENCO's expertise in helping to *extend the range of learning strategies* which was the most widely endorsed strategy. In other words, in the majority of schools the heads saw the SENCO almost as a professional tutor for differentiation, whose expertise in learning methods and differentiated materials could be used by other teachers. This approach was also endorsed by senior managers in the majority of secondary schools, even if it was slightly less common. Only about one-third of the schools, in either phase, said SEN staff were supporting initiatives for gifted pupils, reflecting the widespread assumption that special educational needs are mainly related to low achievement.

♦ One case-study primary school *(Windmill Primary)* relied on its SENCO to be the catalyst, and the disseminator of good practice in differentiation. Lesson observation had been undertaken by the SENCO, who identified areas where practice could be more differentiated. As a result of this, the senior management team was now making their own investigation into classroom practice in particular subject areas. Materials and advice were then advertised around the school as being available from the SENCO, if it was requested by any member of staff. Individual advice and guidance was then forthcoming from the SENCO, but it was not proactively provided for the whole school. One of the senior managers (who was also the INSET coordinator) thought the school needed whole-school INSET to update them on methods of differentiation and assessment.

Secondary schools, with their larger staffs and departmental structures perhaps had greater opportunities for developing this advisory role.

♦ In one secondary *(Headland High)* part of the job description of the Learning Support Coordinator read as follows: 'to assist in the department's programme of introducing and reviewing differentiation within Schemes of Work and associated resourcing'. Feedback from an OFSTED inspection in January 1994 reported that; 'Differentiation – the main focus [of curriculum development work] is commendable.'

Elsewhere, it was noted that pupils in Key Stage 4 achieved greater success in classes where there was in-class learning support. Clearly, this is a school with a commitment to differentiation, using strategies that are appearing to work, and in which the role of the learning Support Department is key.

Two of the secondary schools, however, had taken a policy decision to ask their Learning Support departments to play a leading role in developing differentiation across the school.

♦ In *Rock High* the Learning Development Department had a key role in developing differentiation across the school, helped by a real commitment to improving standards throughout the school from the headteacher and the deputy in charge of pupils' learning. The Learning Development Department was not synonymous with Learning Support – it was a system for all pupils in the school. This was evident in the management structure. The head of the department, a former LEA adviser for SEN, had her own team but also worked closely with senior managers and with subject departments, each of which designated a learning development curriculum coordinator. The LDD did not just offer support in lessons but also had a role in the curriculum organisation and in its delivery. Departments could bid for time to work with the coordinator or her deputy on developing differentiation strategies and for class support (150 periods of support per term, working on a 25 period week). In addition, they were involved in running extension days on a Saturday for various curricular topics, as well as mentoring schemes devised to catch less and more able pupils.

♦ *River High* had a learning support department which had been described in the 1994 OFSTED Inspection Report as a 'model of good practice', achieving high standards in a cost-effective manner and contributing to overall standards. The coordinator of learning support (LS) worked in a curriculum management team comprising eight faculty heads, thus emphasising the importance of the role. She had her own LS curriculum team composed of representatives from each faculty and meeting about four times a term. Their job, (in addition to responsibility for pupil support) was to work on curriculum initiatives in their department and to offer professional development support to colleagues. The coordinator had also had time over the previous three years to work with two departments each year, on differentiating schemes of work. She had also initiated the school's scheme of setting core targets for each pupil to aim for in Key Stage 3. In practice, departments varied in their commitment to the approach and in their readiness to work systematically on differentiation, but the coordinator felt progress was being made. All this development work proceeded alongside the in-class support system which she managed, through six pupil support teachers (non-teaching assistants).

These schools demonstrated that it was indeed possible to move the role of the SENCO to centre stage, as a specialist in learning development, but only when senior managers had taken a strategic decision to do this, and to ensure that the coordinator was brought into the planning team. Furthermore, colleagues were needed within each subject (or year) team, to create a powerful development group. Nevertheless, even when the structures and resources (in staff non-contact time) were in place, it could still be uphill work to persuade other middle managers that this support was an asset rather than some kind of invasion of their professional territory.

Professional development

The case-study schools varied considerably in the way they had structured professional development on differentiation for their staff. To some extent, this reflected the maturity of their differentiation strategy. The practice described above, where systematic in-house development through departments was a continuing process, was the outcome of a number of years of INSET events and projects, which other schools were working through. In the survey, whole-school INSET on differentiation was reported by nearly two-thirds of secondary senior managers as being effective as a strategy for implementing school policy on differentiation. Sending key personnel out on courses was also seen as being effective.

♦ *Causeway High* had a whole-school INSET day on differentiation, which was a mixture of in-house expertise disseminated among other staff members, and outside speakers to talk about the theory and practice of differentiation.

♦ *Headland High* had sent a number of key staff out on courses related to differentiation, most of which were subject-specific, but a number of which were explicitly to do with differentiation. The school had also proposed a detailed outline for an INSET day for the whole school on differentiation in the SDP, including specifying outside speakers.

♦ *Hillside High* brought in outside consultants to participate in the staff development process in relation to differentiation. This proved to be a useful focus for further in-school work on differentiation.

♦ On a smaller scale, dissemination of good practice was evidenced in *Windmill Primary*, where a successful Reading Recovery Scheme in Year 4 was being tried out in other areas of the school.

♦ In *Observatory Primary,* expertise was disseminated throughout the school among staff and pupils in dealing with laptop computers. Pupils were often able to advise teachers on using the machines, which was also perceived by staff to be very good for their self-esteem and development.

Given the stress on teacher expertise, and the focus on differentiation within the classroom, it might be expected that managers would invest heavily in professional development on differentiation. For this reason, the survey investigated a range of approaches.

School managers were asked about the proportion of staff who had taken part in courses which had had either a direct or indirect relevance to differentiation. Figure 5.15 shows the proportion of primary schools and secondary departments where all or some staff had participated in a differentiation course.

Of these four groupings, science departments were the most likely to have had staff on such courses. The lower proportions for primary schools probably reflects the continuing difficulty in creating time for staff to go on courses. Drawing on both parts of the question, we can estimate the proportions of schools or departments with either specific differentiation courses or courses in which differentiation played a part. On this basis, over three-quarters of the primary schools and of each department could report some participation in INSET related to differentiation. About half the schools gave details of the *most helpful strategies for implementing differentiation* which had been derived from such courses. The variety in the responses is yet another reminder of the broad remit of differentiation, as perceived by experienced teachers.

Figure 5.15   Proportion of staff taking part in differentiation course

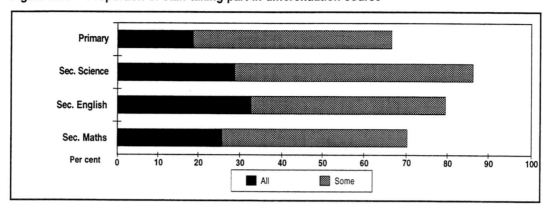

Table 5.3   Types of differentiation-related strategy derived from courses, as suggested by respondents (as a percentage of all responses given)

Focus of most helpful strategies	Maths %	English %	Science %	Primary %
Planning (*whole-school, medium/short-term, teaching/learning policy, setting realistic objectives, varying tasks/roles/targets, reviewing units of work*)	37	27	22	43
Specific strategies (*readability, classroom management, use of IEPs, individual needs analysis*)	19	27	38	17
Resources (*deployment of support staff, developing/selecting materials, extension work*)	11	18	19	10
Awareness raising (*on differentiation, on pupil needs, on NC levels*)	17	11	15	16
Assessment (*relating it to differentiation, planning into topics, moderation*)	4	5	7	22
Staff collaboration (*across subjects, working with support staff*)	7	2	1	12
Other	5	18	14	6
N (number giving any response)	89	109	136	196
As a percentage of all respondents	49	66	72	48

A total of 530 respondents gave some response to this question.
Percentage of responses given within each subject group or by primary heads.

As Table 5.3 suggests, it could cover almost anything connected with effective teaching and learning.

The responses suggest that what middle and senior managers found useful from any courses related to differentiation were strategies that helped them with planning their work and those which provided new tools to use, such as the DART system (Directed Activities Related to Text) or ideas for classroom management. Specific strategies were particularly important to science. Only primary schools were likely to mention assessment-related INSET as relevant to differentiation, in keeping with their perception of the importance of assessment in this context.

Appraisal and monitoring

While senior managers could readily describe and discuss staff development in differentiation, it was much more difficult to pin down their methods for reviewing the effect of their policies on teaching and learning practice. One route, only taken by one or two schools, was to use pupil performance data to investigate 'added value'; but this was only relevant for older pupils. To some extent, responsibility for reviewing classroom practice was devolved to middle managers (heads of department or year team leaders), through review meetings or, where teaching was shared, informal observation of teaching. Only one of the schools had a regular and systematic system of classroom observation and review.

♦ At *Rock High,* one of the key factors was the time given by the SMT for cover, so that subject heads of department could regularly go into classrooms to monitor teaching and learning. At these times, senior managers themselves would free the observers by taking their classes. The aim of the process was to develop a rigorous and effective teaching 'culture' within each department.

Other case-study schools, at a less advanced stage in their development, had begun this process, having devoted SMT time to observing a similar number of lessons a week.

An increasing number of the case-study schools were expressing their commitment to procedures for monitoring teaching quality, and in particular the quality of differentiation. However, appraisal was not an explicit part of any of these procedures, and indeed appraisal was not necessarily related to differentiation unless this was an area specified by the appraisee. The guidelines for appraisal produced by nearly all the LEAs approached through our telephone survey included classroom observation by the appraiser, and they felt that differentiation would therefore be part of the agenda, but teacher interviews suggested that this did not seem to follow. In the survey, only one-fifth of secondary schools and one-third of the primary respondents reported that differentiation was an aspect of their staff appraisal checklist. However, about six out of every ten schools gave a view on the value of their staff appraisal system as a part of their differentiation strategy. Relative to other approaches, it was one of the less effective, especially in secondary schools. Perhaps this reflects the difficulty of discussing the impact of teaching; as one LEA adviser put it, 'Teachers are quite happy to talk in appraisal about the quality of teaching – they are not so confident on the quality of learning or standards of assessment.'

At the time of the study, what seemed to be lacking in the case-study schools was a systematic programme to monitor the quality of both teaching and learning, and its effectiveness in terms of differentiation. While managers could and did monitor the procedures – for example, that departments had handbooks and that (where relevant) they contained appropriate statements on differentiation – it was much harder to evaluate what actually happened in the classroom.

5.4   Towards a Learning Development Strategy

In this chapter we have considered how much responsibility senior managers have for developing, implementing and evaluating a differentiation strategy. There is little doubt that, just as they recognise the importance of differentiation and its link with raising attainment, so they would expect to take the lead in defining the strategy and building the means to put it into effect.

What has come over from the case study and survey evidence is the very real difficulties schools have had in building a comprehensive and coherent strategy for differentiation. There have undoubtedly been notable advances on a number of fronts. These include: raising awareness of differentiation issues through INSET; the development of differentiation principles and guidelines for whole-school and departmental documents; the development of pupil grouping systems intended to target teaching more effectively to pupil needs; the development or refinement of assessment systems to provide better data and feedback on pupils' learning; the use of SEN staff to support and develop teachers' skills in meeting individual needs; the creation of staffing structures and groups to monitor and develop differentiated approaches to learning.

It has become apparent how long it takes to define and implement a strategy of this kind. One primary school deputy stressed that it had taken five years to build year group teams able to work closely together in planning and teaching to meet needs at a range of ability levels. One of the secondary schools was still implementing its 1992 strategy, which had taken some time to evolve. A powerful lever in the hands of managers, to speed up this process once it was under way, was the news of an impending OFSTED inspection. But although this could act as a catalyst in ensuring procedures and documentation relating to differentiation were in place, longer term incentives were needed for the real culture change that was just becoming evident in some of the schools.

This change was revealing because it pointed up some of the reasons why schools have had difficulty with implementing a differentiation strategy and suggested an alternative approach to the same underlying goal of raising the attainment of all pupils. It suggests that, too often, differentiation has in practice focused on remedial arrangements to deal with the shortcomings of the less successful (and possibly the extra demands of the most able). Thus grouping arrangements, teaching resources and the services of the SEN specialists have all been harnessed to this important but essentially compensatory purpose.

In the more exciting contexts, the scenario was being steadily but dramatically transformed, by focusing instead on the common issue of what makes for effective learning – for all pupils. This was evident in all aspects of the management strategy, with two key notes: better 'intelligence' – that is, information on how and what pupils are learning, and what works in the classroom – and more rigorous, self-critical and collaborative professionalism.

6. LESSONS FOR LEARNING: REFLECTING ON THE EVIDENCE

We have now reviewed the principles and practice of differentiation from a number of perspectives, including those of pupils, teachers and managers within schools, LEA staff and those who seek to influence practice through research, training and expertise. This evidence was obtained mainly in 1995, although we have recently contacted case-study schools again for an update on their differentiation practice. In this chapter we want to reflect on what we have learned, drawing on evidence about how things were and about any recent changes in practice. This will help us to identify the findings which remain relevant to what schools are doing and planning now, when the policy context has changed considerably but perhaps teaching and learning arrangements and processes in many schools have changed less.

6.1 Learning from the Evidence

Ten years ago, discussion of differentiation was difficult because the term itself was not much used. When it was, it was either in rather specialist areas such as public examinations, where the concept of 'differentiated papers' was gaining hold in some subjects, among SEN specialists, or in academic debates in educational sociology. By the time we started this study, there had been an enormous change. Almost everyone we asked was familiar with the term and had thought about differentiation as an educational concept. We found an apparent consensus, that differentiation was (or should be) about matching learning to the needs of the individual – as a way of raising attainment – and that it applied to all pupils, not just those with special needs. Now, improvement in learning is more often being discussed using the language of target-setting and school effectiveness. But before we conclude that differentiation has had its day – another passing fad – we need to understand both the achievements and the challenges and contradictions that emerged as schools worked to put differentiation principles into practice.

Achieving long-term change

Some schools have been working at a differentiation programme for up to ten years, starting with awareness-raising INSET days, moving on to small-scale initiatives within teams or departments, building differentiation targets into the SDP, harnessing the skills of SEN staff in staff development, and working through the implications, for other related aspects of practice (such as assessment) and for other groups, such as parents and non-teaching staff. Such a school has 'lived' the change in definitions and priorities that reflects, and is reflected in, the wider policy changes at national level. One of the case-study secondary schools, *Rock High,* demonstrates this process (Box 1), with further evolution in the last two years of some initiatives we saw in 1995, and new moves to promote the underlying goals of professional development and effective whole-school systems to support teaching and learning.

One primary case-study school has used the last two years to consolidate its long-term differentiation approach, based on complex pupil grouping structures. Under its very experienced head teacher, the staff at *Abbey Primary* have refined and extended teaching in setted groups, across a year group. Working in teams to plan their schemes of work, all the Key Stage 2 staff now split the year group into three ability sets for the core subjects; moreover, there are three levels of work (for more able, average and those who need reinforcing) within each set, giving a total of nine levels. Furthermore, the head has introduced 'streaming' for the carousel (foundation subjects) for the current Year 5, to provide generous support for the large numbers of SEN pupils in that year group. He feels that after eight years in the school he has now achieved his goal of getting all the staff to work effectively in teams, so that there is greater consistency. He has used the achievement of the Investors in People award as a lever in developing an 'effective workforce', with a focus on the highest quality of teaching.

Box 1:   Rock High, 1995-97

Already in 1995/96 the school had shifted their language from 'differentiation' to 'learning development', with the lead being taken by SEN staff acting as developers with departments, and staff had accepted classroom observation by senior staff and the involvement of parents in regular discussion of pupil progress. The curriculum programme was gradually being transformed into a pattern of carefully planned modules with material at various levels and explicit learning targets. In the 1997-98 school year, there were signs of further evolution rather than dramatic change. The SENCO had become (acting) deputy head, with responsibility for staff development. The development programme is task-related, linked to SDP priorities and focusing on the management of learning – effective management of classrooms and class time, pupil grouping, assessment. The new appraisal system was developed by a staff working party, not senior managers, and is department-focused, with practical targets, such as (for younger staff) training in marking procedures. This builds on the regular observation and monitoring which is now embedded in departmental practice. The head teacher sees all this as one aspect of the long-term strategy; 'we had already recognised the need to break down differentiation into its component parts – such as pace, high expectations, whole-school priorities, staff development.' One aspect of this strategy is the drive to improve the quality and value of data on pupil progress. In 1996 they were already involved in an externally managed value-added programme. In 1997-98, this continues, and has proved its worth in pointing up action for departments, individual teachers and pupils. But he sees it as 'essentially summative', telling the school about what has happened with cohorts of pupils who have now gone through. The school is therefore beginning to develop 'formative' systems for assessing performance – for example, from entry (SAT scores, analysed alongside CAT results) to Year 7 end of year exam results. They are working on progression from primary into Year 7, so that with better information they can avoid the classic standstill and 'hit the ground running'. Each pupil now has his or her achievement summarised on a single A4 key data sheet accessible to all teachers. Now their next INSET is on how to assess against learning objectives, and they want to set individual learning targets for Year 7 pupils (they are already established for Year 10 and 11). Mentoring initiatives are being extended down the school from Year 11 to Year 10 and for a special project for boys in Year 8. Indeed, target setting includes a scheme for using setting to 'promote' some Key Stage 3 boys into higher sets in order to raise expectations and get them to achieve. Initiatives linked to differentiation which were there in 1996 have been extended; for example, after-school profiling sessions with parents and pupils are now being more closely focused on current subject targets, extension work (on Saturdays and after school) now includes the Big Breakfast Club (a free breakfast for early birds who come to work before classes start). All this is very much 'work in progress', in a school which is growing numerically and is still working on improving the formal outcomes of 'league table' results. The head feels optimistic, perhaps because he is confident about his staff team: 'We've built an open approach here, with trust between staff. It means they can accept professional review, with the continuing and shared aim of improving quality.'

Changes and challenges

In some other schools, changes in leadership were bringing into question some of the approaches we observed during the study. For example, *Cottage Primary* was beginning to change its strategy with the arrival of a new head (Box 2). Moreover his early evaluation suggested that the previous head's passionate commitment to developing pupils as autonomous learners, as a key element of the school's differentiation approach, was perhaps not delivering the linked goal of raising attainment. He saw a need to change structures (for example, to reduce the age-spread within classes) as well as to focus more clearly on standards.

Box 2: Cottage Primary, 1995-97

The new head, who started in September 1997, is forming the view that the system which had been developed to promote pupil self-management in a two-class school, while a valuable tool for classroom organisation, is not necessarily promoting more effective learning. Again, the school roll is growing, and his goal is to move from the current three classes to four, which he feels is the minimum number to permit effective teaching. He is currently engaged in an audit of all aspects of learning, with the aim of setting more clearly defined learning targets, for year groups and for individuals. One of his main goals is to work towards eradicating learning problems during Key Stage 1, so that special needs in Key Stage 2 – currently considerable – become more manageable, and there is more scope to challenge the more able pupils.

At *Hillside High* they were awaiting a new head and were working to build on earlier developments in very challenging circumstances of continuing budget deficits and staffing losses. They had responded very positively to the challenge, with a renewed and more unified drive to focus all their energies on raising attainment through more effective learning (Box 3).

What these glimpses of schools suggest is that the increasingly sharp focus on attainment, through league tables (now at Key Stage 2 as well as Key Stage 4), through OFSTED inspections, through the focus on school effectiveness and target setting, and throughout the sections of *Excellence in Schools* (GB. P. HofC, 1997), is requiring all schools to find practical, effective strategies for implementing that familiar school aim of maximising the potential of every pupil. For some schools, this is what differentiation has always meant, and they have perhaps now changed the terms they use while building on sound foundations. For others, perhaps, differentiation was more of a bandwagon, driven by a few enthusiasts, with the majority picking up only those aspects which met their immediate needs, usually relating to the challenge of teaching lower ability pupils. What lessons can be learned, therefore, from the evidence collected in this study, about putting differentiation into practice in schools, and the impact this seemed to have on raising attainment for all pupils?

Box 3: Hillside High, 1995-97

The senior managers had used the lever of an OFSTED inspection to ensure that all departments completed unitised schemes of work, with built-in targets and levels. The SMT had invested a lot of time working with departments to bring this about, some needing more support than others. They are now '90% confident' that these schemes of work and the associated differentiated delivery are now really happening in the classroom, not just on paper. The banding system has been retained and they are trying to improve information on Year 7 entrants. The real development has been to bring together assessment and learning. The ICA system has now been transformed into a common subject-based assessment scheme, with target-setting at the start of each unit. Pupils are given a 'higher' or 'foundation' target at this stage, through individual or small-group negotiation, and progress is assessed against this. Subject teachers also have training providers produce a Personal and Social Qualities profile, which consists of ten items, focusing on the management of learning. Five times a year each teacher has to supply a subject assessment on each pupil for the central database, currently being implemented, which will mean up-to-date information on progress across the curriculum will be available for each pupil. At present, these developments are starting with Key Stage 3, while efforts are made to raise the very low expectations of many Key Stage 4 pupils, a feature of the economically depressed area in which they live. An exercise to assess current and potential GCSE performance for Year 11 suggests a gap to be bridged of up to 25 per cent. In general, teaching and learning has become the major focus for the school, with appraisal for all staff focusing on this. They have appointed a senior teacher as Assessment Manager to drive the whole programme forward, improving the quality of learning and promoting the greater consistency across departments which OFSTED had advocated.

We shall first (6.2) review the main findings, linked to the three key groups – pupils, teachers and managers – and then consider some underlying issues which emerge from these findings, and which help to explain why differentiation has proved a problematic challenge for schools (6.3). Finally, in 6.4, we shall suggest some ways of applying the lessons we have learned to the current policy context.

6.2 School Perspectives on Differentiation: Pupils, Teachers, Managers

In reviewing what has been learned from the contributions of pupils, teachers and managers to differentiation practice, we should like to revisit some of the ideas put forward in Chapter 2 and 3.

The conversations with, and observations of, *pupils* at work suggested that they have useful and perceptive comments to make about what helps them to learn. There was evidence that they were relatively dependent on the teacher, both for organising their work and for help in carrying it out. And yet, there were plenty of indications that pupils could and did organise themselves effectively, supported each other in their work and made suggestions about how to carry it forward – all these developments being more likely to occur, on the whole, in Key Stage 2 than in Key Stage 3 classrooms.

What seemed to be missing was instruction in the relevant skills of managing their own learning and the art of working productively with others; and, indeed, a climate in which it was natural to make learning targets explicit and to spell out the criteria for success. They appreciated the feedback of one-to-one review from the teacher, but were mostly unsure about self-assessment, working out their place in the class 'pecking order' from external indicators. The survey data showed that secondary teachers were rather less likely than their primary colleagues to see self-assessment and various other forms of participation as relevant to their (Key Stage 3) pupils, and also less likely to judge their pupils as competent in these skills.

Turning to the *teachers'* perspective, we reviewed what teachers believe are the priorities for classroom differentiation, how they plan their work to put these principles into action and the way they respond to pupils' needs in the classroom. There were differences between the data on differentiation strategies obtained from lesson observation and from the survey, with observed practice failing to match the level of usage reported in the survey.

In a wide variety of school and classroom settings, a great deal of work had been done to plan tasks and materials for varying levels of ability, to accommodate different learning styles and in some cases to define clear and explicit learning targets. There was more chance of involving all departments or staff teams where there was clear pressure and support from senior managers.

It proved more difficult to feel confident about what was being achieved through differentiation strategies in the classroom. Teachers were expected to adapt schemes of work or differentiated modules to fit their own classes, but this was usually done incrementally, as they got to know their pupils, rather than on the basis of diagnostic assessment. Many prepared variations to a common task or theme, with the variation usually related to ability and encapsulated in written materials – often at three 'levels'. Only a minority of teachers offered a variety of resource types, response modes or pupil roles. A few schools had made major progress in planning and managing their in-class support.

In addition to the many practical problems, we identified two more fundamental issues about delivering differentiation. First, many teachers were working hard but not effectively enough, even within their own agreed principles. Secondly, and relatedly, most schools and teachers were only just developing a shared professional language in which to discuss achievement, among themselves and with their pupils. There was also the issue of whether they were being effective enough in enlisting pupils actively into the learning process. In primary schools, this was the goal but there seemed to be some confusion about how it was to serve the purpose of raising attainment. However, in Key Stage 3, in too many instances, pupils were often expected to play a much more passive and conformist role. The 'cost' of this relative failure to enlist pupils fully in the learning process was to make the teacher's task, of knowing the pupils and meeting individual needs, proportionately harder.

The second issue concerned the development of a common language of achievement. Although 'responding flexibly' was at the top of the teachers' list of practicable differentiation strategies, it proved quite difficult to discuss with teachers, partly because it was 'automatic', part of their ordinary repertoire, and partly because there was often not a readily used vocabulary for discussing teaching and learning methods. It was suggested that such a vocabulary was also needed for a language for sharing assessment criteria more readily with pupils and strengthening the perceived value of learning support staff.

Finally, we considered the responsibility which senior and middle managers have for developing, implementing and evaluating a differentiation strategy. The case study and survey evidence pointed to the very real difficulties schools have had in building a comprehensive and coherent strategy for differentiation and the length of time this takes, especially to achieve the real culture change that was just becoming evident in some of the schools. Instead, differentiation had often focused on remedial arrangements to deal with the shortcomings of the less successful (and possibly the extra demands of the most able).

Pupil management had focused recently on grouping by ability, which the survey confirmed had increased in recent years for most age groups. It was proving harder to design and implement common and transparent pupil assessment systems, to help teachers to 'know their pupils' and what they could do more accurately; and also to develop a strategy to encourage pupils to take more responsibility for their learning.

While heads and senior managers were heavily involved in leading the differentiation strategy, middle managers also played an important role, particularly in secondary schools. Here, heads of department were expected to shoulder much of the responsibility, and felt they got rather little practical support in return. A more coherent approach, evident in two schools, was to give a central role to the SENCO, redefined as a learning specialist and commissioned to create a framework in which subject departments were expected to operate.

Although there had been a variety of INSET on differentiation, usually starting with a whole-day event for all the staff, practical help with planning for differentiation or specific strategies for use in the classroom was most appreciated. It was relatively rare for differentiation to have been tied in to the appraisal system in any structured way,

Some schools were now focusing instead on the common issue of what makes for effective learning – for all pupils, rather than on differentiation. This was evident in all aspects of the management strategy, with two key notes: better 'intelligence' – that is, information on how and what pupils are learning, and what works in the classroom – and more rigorous, self-critical and collaborative professionalism.

In Chapter 2, we presented a diagram (Figure 2.5) which aimed to represent the dynamic character of learning, and the roles of the three groups in the process. It suggested that teachers and pupils have to engage actively with each other in the learning process, and with the requirements of the learning task, defining and using appropriate targets, resources, strategies and dialogue. The role of the managers is principally as facilitators and agenda setters.

The evidence we have gathered seems in keeping with this model, but suggests that the process has to be more sustained and more strongly directed than that diagram suggested. As the questions in Figure 3.1 indicate, it has become apparent that we are talking about redirecting or re-focusing the school as a whole onto learning. The handicap so far is that using 'differentiation' as the banner under which to mount this campaign has created some daunting and perhaps redundant obstacles. In the rest of this chapter we shall discuss this idea, and its implications for current and future policy.

6.3 Hard Lessons: Differentiation under Challenge

Is differentiation an impossible dream?

Behind the comments and explanations given by many teachers seemed to lie a rather wistful recognition that differentiation was an ideal which fitted their educational aims but which in practice could never be implemented in real classrooms. Instead, there were halfway solutions which at least addressed the challenge and were as much as could be managed. This response could be labelled 'differentiation as a dream', and there seemed to be two versions of it. One focused on the individual learner, and the concept of matching learning to individual needs. In an ideal world, classes would be of a size where this would be feasible; or there would be sufficient adults to provide a similarly high adult-pupil ratio. As one teacher saw it, this might just be managed for the special needs group, but even a special school with higher staff-pupil ratios felt individual matching was a major challenge. The other version of the differentiation dream was based on a different interpretation, which stressed diversity rather than match and might be termed 'entitlement through diversity'. Here diversity applied not only to pupils (in ability, personality, family support and many other factors) but to learning styles, teaching approaches, curriculum requirements, assessment methods and many other facets of classroom management. As one commentator has put it, 'differentiation needs to be perceived in terms of entitlement to as full and flexible a curriculum as possible and to be thought of in terms of how the curriculum might cater for and build on diversity' (Bearne, 1996). The ideal might be somewhat unfairly termed 'let a thousand flowers bloom', and it is not entirely surprising that the quotation comes from a collection of papers on primary education, in which differentiation is linked with diversity in the title as well as the substance of the book. Here also is a demanding ideal for teachers who ideally want to offer a rich experience which will allow all pupils to benefit and to progress.

The risk of seeing differentiation as an impossible (or nearly impossible) dream is that teachers either dismiss it or, more probably, work on what is seen as a practicable, if compromise strategy. The terms of this strategy can reveal more about what are seen to be the defining aspects of differentiation, and thus about teachers' priorities for the management of learning. We shall therefore consider each of the versions of the 'dream' which we have outlined: differentiation as 'individual match' or as 'entitlement through diversity'.

Differentiation as individual match. The Scottish study of differentiation practice in primary schools (Simpson, 1989; Simpson *et al.*, 1989) investigated in depth and with considerable rigour the hypothesis of differentiation as match. The results demonstrated that, in the terms they had defined, even the experienced teachers, recognised as 'good differentiators' by their colleagues, had some difficulty in matching tasks to pupils' measured capabilities. In particular, they were likely to underestimate the competence of the more able pupils. Attempts to crack this problem are most commonly found in individualised maths programmes, which provide carefully structured routes with remedial and practice loops to fit individual performance profiles. But the problems of sustaining individualised programmes are well known – loss of motivation, difficulties with pace and practice and still no guarantee of 'match' for all pupils. More recently an intensive effort to offer individualised and interactive tuition in maths and some aspects of literacy has been made through the use of computer-based Integrated Learning Systems, but although there were early signs of significant learning gains in some contexts (NCET, 1994, 1996), there is as yet no evidence that this approach offers a cost-effective way of consistently raising attainment through 'match'.

In most subjects, and for most teachers, the goal is less ambitious – not to pre-plan materials, tasks or learning routes to provide a precise or individualised match, but at least to plan learning to satisfy a range of pupil capabilities. The difficulty here is the need to simplify the task in line with practical constraints – principally lack of time and resources. In our study, the most common response, in both primary and secondary schools, was to define three categories or levels, and prepare schemes of work, or materials to fit them. While the approach might differ – for example, it might involve three 'levels' of worksheet, or materials to fit the 'must/should/could' framework – it implied defining tasks not in terms of the assessed capabilities of actual pupils but for normative groups of pupils – for example, more able, average, less able. Of course, differentiation of materials in this way is in itself a major undertaking, and may well increase access and challenge for many pupils, especially in the hands of a skilful teacher. However, the fit with individual needs may remain rough and ready, with further dangers of discrimination and labelling.

There seem to be several problems with the dream of 'match'. Given the diversity of pupils' capabilities, even where these are accurately defined – itself a major challenge –and the realities of classroom management, achieving 'match' with any consistency is always going to be extremely challenging. One of our schools *(Abbey Primary)* has now taken the approach about as far as is feasible, through a combination of setting, in-class grouping by level, team planning and specialist teaching. But most of the teachers we spoke to saw setting and other pupil-grouping strategies as only a very partial solution, given the diversity (of ability and other characteristics) within any group or class.

Differentiation as diversity. A very different interpretation stressed the importance of diversity, not only in demonstrating the need for differentiation but also in planning classroom responses. There is a link here with a strong commitment to entitlement. If pupils differ in so many ways, it is argued, only a rich diversity in learning materials and approaches is likely to secure entitlement to the curriculum. One version of this approach (Doddington, 1996) is based on a constructivist view of learning, in which 'the suggestion is that thinking and genuine understanding can occur only through active engagement and processes of interpretation'. Differentiation as diversity was less common in our study, but there were signs of the approach in some primary classes. Sometimes this was the result of classroom management strategies, for example when pupils were all following their own schedules at *Cottage Primary*, so that the teacher could maximise the time spent with pupils on basic skills, particularly maths teaching. In other schools and classes, diversity not only in activities but also in approaches and the specific nature of tasks was actually the outcome of skilful and flexible planning and response by an experienced teacher. But there were other settings where diversity – in what pupils were doing and achieving – was actually nearer to confusion, with little indication that pupils were benefiting. If too mechanistic an interpretation of 'match' may constrain learning, well-meaning attempts to assess and provide for different learning styles and multiple forms of intelligence seem likely to cause problems in the hands of all but the most experienced teacher.

Behind both these scenarios lies an assumption that pupils' education would benefit if only the dream could be realised: more, or better differentiation is the goal. But there is another view, that the ultimate goal would be to eliminate much of the need for differentiation, as it is now practised. The argument is that much differentiation is in practice a form of compensatory education, to cope with some pupils' accumulated skills deficit, and consequent lack of motivation. This view, put forward by several primary head teachers in recent discussions, is in line with current strategies outlined in the White Paper to focus particularly on effective progress for all in the early years, and is already being reflected in home-school programmes, extra support in Key Stage 1 and literacy initiatives. If the current literacy and numeracy targets can be reached, it would certainly shift the focus of practice and priorities linked to differentiation away from compensation, allowing teachers to explore a variety of ways of improving the fit between learner, task and resources.

Differentiation and diagnosis: 'knowing the pupils'

Whatever their interpretation, teachers with a commitment to differentiation agreed that the essential precondition for any strategy was 'knowing the pupils'. Until the teacher knew the pupils in her class, it was said to be impossible to plan learning to meet their needs. While this was generally accepted, therefore, as a *sine qua non*, particularly by experienced teachers, it was more difficult to pin down what it meant. The same principle has been found in studies of progression, particularly from primary to secondary education, as in a recent NFER project, Effective Progression from Primary to Secondary Schooling (see Schagen and Kerr, forthcoming). Secondary school staff will talk about getting to know their new entrants, during the first half-term, before making decisions about grouping or setting, or indeed other measures to tailor the curriculum to individuals. What are the essential processes or forms of evidence that teachers need before they feel confident that they know their pupils? Above all, it seems, more important than any written records or assessments, is the process of personal interaction: working with pupils, seeing how they respond in the classroom, getting acquainted with them as social beings as well as learners. Only then does the written record, the evidence provided by others who have already worked with the pupil in other classrooms or schools, become significant. By that stage, the teacher can evaluate the written evidence against what s/he 'knows' about the pupil. At the same time, just because the pupil is 'known', the evidence of others may be seen as redundant. Of course, there are exceptions to this, not least the careful joint scrutiny by secondary and primary SENCOs of Year 6 pupils with special needs preparing for transfer to secondary school. Nevertheless, the great majority of teachers we interviewed stressed the importance of building up this personal, multi-dimensional knowledge that could only be acquired from direct contact with pupils, usually in the classroom.

The distinction can more easily be expressed by the two French verbs, *savoir* and *connaître*. What these teachers seem to mean is *connaître*, they need to become acquainted with their pupils, to know them as people, to understand, to appreciate them and to diagnose any specific difficulties they may have. Compared with that, it appears, knowing *(savoir)* things about the pupil such as test scores or even the interpretations of other professionals, 'knowing that' s/he can (or cannot) perform certain tasks, understands specific concepts or has studied particular topics, is of secondary significance. It is difficult to gainsay the value of a hard-won, experiential understanding of each learner. At the same time, why is it that teachers apparently find it hard, or are reluctant, to make full use of prior evidence about pupils? Primary teachers who will have the major or sole charge of their class can have some confidence that they will indeed get to know *(connaître)* all the pupils in their class, although it may take some weeks. For some secondary teachers who teach hundreds of pupils in a week, this level of 'knowledge' may indeed seem an impossible dream.

The issue which, from our case-study evidence, seemed to need further discussion was how professionally valid measures could be developed to speed up the process. In other words, the challenge relates to the nature of the assessment evidence that is available, the assessment language and concepts that teachers share, and the extent to which one teacher can 'read' and trust the evidence provided by others, as a basis for planning, from the outset, appropriate teaching and learning for the diversity of pupils in each class. There are two issues here. The first, following from what has been said above, is the need most teachers feel to make their own assessment, rather than relying on others' judgements. The second concerns the challenge of using assessment tools to embody and express knowledge relevant to a pupil's learning; in other words to apply diagnostic assessment, as a systematic part of professional practice. The extent to which this was done seemed to depend on a number of factors: it was more likely to occur when SEN staff were involved, for certain curriculum areas (especially literacy and numeracy in primary schools, maths, foreign languages and some science courses in secondary schools), or where the school had developed common assessment criteria and systems.

From these two issues flow two challenges. The first is to develop and continue to expand a professionally appropriate and accessible assessment language for describing pupils' capabilities and weaknesses, in terms which are valid, specific and can be effectively shared with all colleagues who need to know. The process of moderation of NCA outcomes among staff within a department or a school or – more demandingly – among teachers from different schools or phases – has done much to address this challenge. As a result, definitions – with examples – of what constitutes satisfactory performance on a particular task have become more specific and also, importantly, are shared and understood by groups of teachers from different backgrounds. Nevertheless, continuing concern about whether a Key Stage 2 Level 4 or 5 can possibly be equivalent to a Key Stage 3 Level 4 or 5 suggests that it is not just a matter of clearer definitions but also of trust between colleagues working in different contexts.

The second challenge is, if anything, even more demanding, because it concerns the use of assessment results in the planning and implementation of schemes of work – feeding back assessments into teaching, as the concept of diagnostic assessment implies. It was easier to see this process at work in primary classrooms, where the class teacher had a daily opportunity to feed back observations on progress or learning difficulties into the work programme, particularly in language and number work. Some degree of diagnostic assessment was also built into certain maths schemes. More often, however, test results and grades for written work were summative in nature, a record of performance. The feedback process was more readily observable within the classroom, as the informal but highly skilled set of responses which experienced teachers apply in questioning pupils within the course of a lesson.

Easing the burden of differentiation

Perhaps not surprisingly, in the light of the issues already identified, differentiation appeared to some, if not as a dream then as an overwhelming burden. Here was a concept backed by OFSTED and numerous government pronouncements which seemed to make impossible demands on the already overstretched teacher. The issue here is whether teachers had perhaps misjudged the extent to which they individually could or should shoulder the whole burden.

First, there is ample evidence, from this study and elsewhere, that working in teams is now accepted practice. It is true in many cases that the teamwork is limited to planning and (maybe) review, rather than teaching and/or observation, but at least the benefits of sharing some aspects of the professional agenda have become much more evident, especially in pooling expertise in teaching and learning methods. In some of our schools, the contribution of SEN professionals to this process was particularly valued. Where departmental or year teams had decided to develop a range of differentiated learning resources, sharing this work out among colleagues was probably the only way to make the task feasible, but it could also prove a valuable form of professional development.

Secondly, there is little doubt that teachers working within a supportive strategic framework, with the backing of senior managers and with clear targets, were more likely to feel committed to working at the challenge of differentiation within their own sphere.

Thirdly, as the recent White Paper (GB. P. HofC, 1997) has pointed out, many schools are using their management of budgets to increase the number of adults other than teachers, to support learning in the classroom. Two of the case-study schools, one primary and one secondary, volunteered in recent interviews that they were not only extending the role of classroom assistants but also ensuring that they had the opportunity of training for an appropriate qualification. Adult helpers may embrace a range of volunteers, from business-based mentors and placements to parents. The development of family literacy initiatives (Brooks, 1996) suggests that the scope for actively involving all parents as partners in the learning enterprise, at least for primary pupils, is considerable, a point which had been recognised and acted on in several of the case-study schools.

Lastly, and most challengingly, how far is it possible to incorporate the pupils themselves as active contributors to planning and managing their own learning? We saw that teachers in our survey, especially in secondary schools, were somewhat sceptical about most pupils' skills in this respect. And yet some primary pupils were clearly competent from quite a young age in the practical management of daily activity schedules; some of them also showed they could tutor other children and accept help from classroom 'experts' (particularly in computer work). One study of paired reading has suggested that pupils particularly appreciated having their peers as tutors, and made good progress (Topping and Whiteley, 1990). Experience from the Technical and Vocational Educational

Initiative and in particular the Flexible Learning initiative (Morris and Twitchen, 1990) demonstrated that it was possible to teach older pupils to manage work units based on a tutorial plus research format, once they had been taught the necessary skills. More generally, by Key Stage 4 pupils are being expected to manage coursework schedules, and to understand and in some schools to work to individual targets based on GCSE grade estimates. Tapping the potential of pupils in these ways seems perhaps the most promising route of all to ease the teacher's burden, if only because of numbers. The extent to which pupils can become a resource, actively contributing to the management of the classroom process, may determine the success of schools' strategy for enhancing learning and raising attainment for all.

Re-focusing priorities

Another reason for seeing differentiation as a burden is even more relevant for the current discussion. There were always problems with the term because of its 'slipperiness' and because of its association (for some) with narrowing of educational opportunities rather than entitlement for all. As the term, and the underlying concepts, became more widely accepted, other problems have arisen. Most importantly, it could be used as a portmanteau term to cover everything that needed to be done to raise attainment through better classroom practice. Thus middle managers could be asked to ensure that their differentiation strategy was written into their planning documents, with little explicit guidance on what that implied. We have suggested that practice in many schools has often been coloured by the stress on 'compensatory' strategies for pupils who have been underachieving from the start.

Included within the 'portmanteau' were a whole range of initiatives to address different aspects of the agenda: from individualised learning resources to extension and enrichment activities; from flexible, resource-based learning to a diversity of pupil-grouping systems. But how were these initiatives to be harnessed to the underlying, and universally endorsed goal of raising attainment, individually and institutionally? What seemed to be needed was a better analysis of what changes were envisaged at every level. As the head of *Rock High* said (Box 1), 'we had already [in 1995] recognised the need to break down differentiation into its component parts – such as pace, high expectations, whole-school priorities, staff development.' Once this process had begun, maybe the term itself would become redundant? Or, more constructively, the goal could be redefined and renamed as effective learning for all. This change would encourage schools to distinguish between differences between pupils (in achievement, understanding and skills) to be challenged and preferences to be explored and encouraged. In other words, as pupils become effective learners, they can continually expand their options of what and how to learn. In considering, in the next section, how to take forward the lessons we have learned from this study of differentiation practice, we therefore focus strongly on what is being, and might be, done to promote effective learning for all, and to challenge unacceptable differences in learning capacity.

6.4   Looking Forward: Effective Learning for All

Within the last year, government pressure and support for raising attainment through school improvement has gathered pace. The publication of the White Paper *Excellence in Schools* (GB. P. HofC, 1997) summarised progress so far and made clear the demands that would be made on schools to contribute to demanding national targets and to set challenging targets of their own.   Making the most of the National Curriculum moratorium, the government has put the emphasis on processes and procedures to improve performance within that framework, under the slogan 'standards, not structures'.   On the face of it, the policy is to review all aspects of schooling and to identify new approaches or ways of improving on current methods, bringing in as many support systems (from the LEA, business and the community) as possible.   But all these initiatives and recommendations add up to nothing less than a revolution in professional practice. From now on, all teachers in all schools will be expected to adopt, within an alarmingly short time scale, the 'best practice' which a small minority of schools and LEAs have been trying out in recent years, often on the basis of many years of self-evaluation and development. If differentiation has proved hard to implement, this will be a challenge of an altogether greater magnitude. The only difference is that, while differentiation has had some official endorsement but no funded development, the new agenda will be very public, and already involves major initiatives by the Department for Education and Employment (DfEE) to identify, evaluate and publicise good practice.

Central to the whole enterprise is the promotion of effective learning (leading to enhanced attainment); and a key component is performance-related target-setting, at all levels – national, local, institutional, group, individual. This makes the strategies for improving practice which we have considered in this study, in relation to differentiation, now much more explicitly the means towards an end: that is, achieving performance-related targets.

Those who have had their awareness raised through differentiation programmes will be very conscious of the many questions raised by this shift. For example, how should targets be set, for a school or for subgroups of pupils, since average performance can mask wide differentials within any cohort? How can schools ensure that justice is done to progress made by pupils, as well as to final standards reached? How will target-setting be translated into curriculum planning and practice? And, above all, what evidence is there that target-setting helps to raise attainment – for all or any pupils? The 'good practice guide' on target-setting (GB. OFSTED/DfEE, 1996) offered some answers to these questions, through the examples of developments in specific schools, but the challenge is still a significant one. The more recent guidance from the Standards and Effectiveness Unit of the DfEE, *From Targets to Action* (GB. DfEE, SEU 1997), spells out with very specific examples how this might be done. However, the main emphasis in the document is on institutional targets. While these will have important implications for individual pupils and may well result in initiatives to support or challenge individuals, the main impact is on senior and middle managers, as they work with staff to establish a target-setting culture for the school's drive to raise attainment. Only a small part of the guide is devoted to pupil targets, with an illuminating reference to a school which felt that standards had risen because they had 'demystified the process of teaching and learning for pupils' through sharing explicit targets with them.

However, the advantage of the new context is that it provides a common goal, which without equivocation can apply to all pupils, in all their diversity. But if this is not to be just a new rhetoric, it will indeed involve major change. In part, this means a change of attitude (challenging expectations), but more importantly – since this is likely to prove a means for achieving that shift – it requires the widespread and continuing development of skills, old and new, by pupils, teachers and managers. 'Learning from differentiation' suggests, we would argue, that this is precisely the agenda that has emerged from this study as both constructive and necessary. In the rest of this chapter we want to focus more specifically on these skills. And, *pace* the White Paper, (which stresses 'standards rather than structure') we will first review briefly the structures, at several levels, that seem most likely to facilitate the development of these skills. The equation for delivering effective learning could be expressed as Skills + Structures = Standards.

Structures to support effective learning

The structures we have in mind are less to do with pupil grouping, whether in sets or more innovative arrangements, than with support systems, above all for professional development and review. Schools dedicated to raising attainment strive to create time for teachers to meet for professional collaboration, to tailor appraisal to fit the requirements of the development plan and to devise opportunities for purposeful one-to-one pupil review. As some of our head teachers said, the secret to building structures that teachers were happy to use was to create a climate of honesty and reciprocity. Since the changes needed may present a direct challenge to professional beliefs and practice, this kind of mutual trust is even more necessary so that target-setting, for example, and the systems devised to support it, are seen as part of the school's agreed strategy and not a bureaucratic imposition.

This study, while recognising the increase in setting over recent years, was not designed to test its impact as a strategy for raising attainment. The most common view was that grouping by ability, however this was done, was a necessary but not sufficient strategy for tailoring learning to pupils' needs. Primary teachers were more likely to comment on its value for 'stretching' more able pupils. Pupil grouping arrangements have to be evaluated for their effectiveness in facilitating rigorous, relevant and effective learning, and this includes watching out for the familiar but insidious effects, on teachers and learners, of 'labelling' individuals and groups. Just as important is the issue of structures and systems for progression, particularly at the transition between key stages and between schools. While this was not a major focus of the present study, it was very apparent that present structures are likely to be dysfunctional for effective learning, with assessments disregarded and a 'fresh start' approach being common. The very fact that national and local structures such as many LEA support services and all OFSTED inspection teams deal with primary *or* secondary schools, and not the 'gap' in-between means this structural issue has not received the attention it deserves.

Mention of local and national structures is a reminder of the increasingly important role LEAs and local and national task forces will have to play in leading and supporting change. Discussions with LEA staff suggest that they, too, are aware of the need for the kind of major investment of professional development that is being proposed for schools, if they are to fulfil their role in developing effective procedures for collecting, analysing and feeding back performance data of sufficient quality. This is just one aspect of the re-skilling process, the major part of which will take place within schools.

Skilling the workforce

Skills of using evidence to analyse and evaluate individual performance. The target-setting agenda makes enormous assumptions about participants' expertise in the use of assessment data of all kinds to analyse performance and use this evidence in order to raise attainment. Probably the most topical and high profile aspect of the agenda is the various forms of value added analyses. The concept of measuring 'value added' by the school, to assess progress as well as outcomes, is well established. The data requirements are also widely understood – that one needs a measure of performance on entry (or some other starting point) to compare with the performance outcome. Furthermore, many secondary schools are assuming a certain form of testing (standardised tests of 'ability') and even a particular test (the Cognitive Abilities Test, Thorndike *et al.*, 1996) as the most appropriate entry measure. Interestingly, this is currently preferred to Key Stage 2 outcomes, either in the form of levels or of scores. In primary schools, it is harder to settle on appropriate entry or outcome measures at present, although the assumption in the White Paper and elsewhere is that National Curriculum Assessment (NCA) will provide these at the end of each stage, together with baseline testing at the reception stage. Meanwhile, many primary schools have increased their use of published tests in recent years. However, schools seemed to expect testing to fulfil many purposes, with the stress on the summative, and it was not clear how far test results were used or shared among the staff team for school self-evaluation.

If testing is to contribute to raising attainment, many questions need to be asked, not only about why certain tests are used, but about how many people see the results, whether they have the training to interpret them, and how far the data can be used to inform current planning. In addition to the technical skills needed to 'read' the analysis, considerable interpretative and interpersonal skills may be needed to identify their significance in specific contexts and to help others to 'learn the lessons'. Even then, this type of evaluation, based on the application of quantitative analyses, illuminating though it can be in the right hands, has to be translated into implications for current and future practice. The head of *Rock High* felt the need for earlier indicators of progress – say from entry to the end of Year 7. Applying formal 'value-added' techniques throughout schooling may prove a step too far, but the idea of equipping all staff with the skills to exploit test scores for evaluating progress and analysing year-on-year patterns of performance and to share the results with colleagues would transform the knowledge base about actual and potential attainment.

While data analysis and interpretation skills are still something of a minority activity, there have been very considerable increases in teachers' assessment expertise, that is in the process of assessing pupil performance, since the introduction of NCA. This has also been extended and consolidated through the professional discourse engendered by moderation, within and between schools. But, as we have seen, the essential requirement in NCA is summative. While many schools have taken the opportunity to use the NCA framework for both internal monitoring and formative review, development has been more uneven.

There is even less indication of systematic programmes to teach pupils how to understand and take an active part in assessment. But there is a long tradition now, going back to the work of the Assessment of Performance Unit (Foxman, Hutchison and Bloomfield, 1991), of strategies for developing a more diagnostic approach to assessing pupils' oral and written performance, which could serve as the basis for helping pupils to be clear about what is required. There has also been work which suggests that pupils can understand and use assessment criteria, and, as a result, develop a more accurate appreciation of their own performance and progress, and know what counts as success in a particular task. Acquiring and exercising these skills is likely to make a more positive contribution to effective learning, through challenging and raising expectations, than the reinforcement of the usual informal pecking order of achievement which pupils invariably work out among their group. There is so far little positive evidence that computer-aided methods of taking pupils through a diagnostic loop, for example in Integrated Learning Systems (Underwood and Brown, 1997), is directly associated with enhanced performance, but there may be scope for using interactive software to develop self-assessment skills and a better understanding of assessment as a feedback process. Nor is this just an exercise for the gifted or average pupil. In fact, the introduction of Individual Education Plans for pupils with SEN may have done more than any other aspect of the SEN Code of Practice to make the assessment expertise of SEN staff accessible to pupils (and their parents) as well as to other teachers. Where learning targets, and performance against them is made explicit to, and discussed with, all those involved, pupils can develop a more realistic understanding of their progress.

Skills of curriculum planning and target setting. Evidence of performance, however sophisticated the analysis, still has to be translated into learning programmes and targets. Here, too, a whole range of skills will be required, if the goal of effective learning for all is to become any kind of reality, and all the participants – pupils, teachers and managers – are involved. At present, the emphasis in policy documents is primarily on institutional targets. Even more challenging is the task of converting these into sectional (departmental, year group) targets and then into targets for subgroups of pupils (boys, the most able) and for individuals. At present, the most likely groups to be set individual targets are some GCSE pupils (especially those on the Grade C/D borderline), and some sixth-form pupils (where value-added analyses have been carried out). In both cases, targets are linked to improving examination grades and may be based on a range of statistical predictions. For younger pupils, where targets are set they may range from the hopelessly flabby (I must improve my spelling) to the misleadingly precise (based on quantitative data only loosely linked to the curriculum). Much more work needs to be done on the skills needed for setting valid and appropriate targets. One approach, at which some teachers have become skilled, is to specify learning objectives for a unit of work, so that pupils can be clear about what they will or should be able to do when they have completed it. This may be an enormous step forward in enabling pupils to realise that there is a goal other than getting through the material. It is very much harder to define valid and appropriate targets for individuals, informed by evidence on their progress to date – although this is a skill which many primary teachers are deploying, even if the procedures are sometimes informal or implicit. One way forward may be to define targets, where appropriate, in performance terms, so that individuals' progress can be tracked, and new targets set, within an agreed framework. Such a detailed specification might only be appropriate for certain key skills and concepts within subject areas, and would need prior analysis and agreement by a teaching team – in itself a challenging task.

Our review of curriculum planning, as described by teachers in case-study schools, suggests that the shift to a systematic target-setting approach would involve teachers in making the link between assessment evidence and planned tasks much clearer. For example, what knowledge, skills, vocabulary, concepts are 'entry requirements' for the task? Have these been assessed, and with what results? What is to be done if some pupils do not have them? Such an approach certainly implies differentiation of methods, tasks or resources in the classroom, but without this, it is very likely that some pupils would make little progress, and indeed would fall further behind. It is still rather different, in making both learning targets and requirements explicit, from the approach of planning support materials and extension opportunities around a core task which is defined – but not necessarily clearly specified – as the norm for what the class should achieve.

Pedagogic skills – making expertise explicit. Teachers may have become used to planning in teams, but very often the collaboration ends there. In some of our schools, staff had made major changes to a rigorous, professional team approach, with regular, structured observation of classrooms by senior or more experienced staff, or by peers, and systematic review based on a range of evidence. Once more, such an approach, if it is to lead to continuous improvement, calls for a wide range of skills: in observation, definition of agreed criteria, development of a language to describe and analyse the pedagogy in use in classrooms, and all the interpersonal skills, trust and honesty to discuss and share one's own practice with others. In such a context, it is possible to move well beyond sterile debates about individualised or whole-class teaching. More than anything, it may make it possible to shift the balance of teacher investment from preparing materials (important though that can be) to talking about and evaluating pedagogy – the heart of the classroom process – and how this can be harnessed to promote effective learning. What can teachers learn from each other, in their own or other schools, about how to vary learning methods and styles to suit the task, purpose and clientele? To maximise time on task? To ensure that homework is not used merely for 'finishing classwork', and that some pupils are not left with every task uncompleted? To make the best possible use of classroom assistants?

Here again, it is not just the teachers who may need to develop these skills. Indeed, their task may become far more manageable when pupils have also been inducted into relevant aspects of pedagogy – or, to use more familiar terms, 'learning to learn' skills. It is highly significant that, among the strategies advocated in the White Paper for 'meeting the different abilities of pupils', is 'the systematic teaching of thinking skills'. Reference is made there to research linking this approach with positive learning outcomes (GB. P.HofC, 1997, p.39). Over a decade ago, this type of approach was a key feature of several projects in the DES's Lower Attaining Pupils Programme. At that stage, the positive outcomes were less clear, partly because the thinking skills modules were too divorced from the mainstream curriculum. But even so, the value of this approach was that it was specifically designed to reduce the impulsiveness which is characteristic of many ineffective learners, and to encourage them to develop conscious strategies for solving cognitive problems. One of the strengths of Shayer's development of the thinking skills strategy was that he embedded the skills within normal science programmes (Adey and Shayer, 1994). The potential value of the approach in our context is that it actually redresses the balance, improving learning effectiveness for many pupils through access to the very strategies which 'successful' students have always had available to them. Other thinking skills techniques, such as concept mapping, all of which need careful teaching, can increase pupils' control over and confidence in the learning process.

Skills in managing learning. Every newly qualified teacher wants, above all, to become a competent classroom manager. But the skills involved are hard won, and it is interesting that younger teachers at *Rock High* wanted their professional development to focus on some of the apparently mundane but very important skills, such as marking and time management within the classroom. If the range of professional skills, in assessment, target-setting and pedagogy is to be extended, and pupils are to be made more active partners in their own learning, then the task of managing the process also becomes more challenging. What skills might be involved? One strand will be pupil-focused: training pupils to manage materials, to retrieve information, to plan and evaluate their work, to adopt a number of roles (as group member, 'expert', tutor, secretary and so on), to negotiate, to collaborate, to review progress. But there will also be the skills of whole-class teaching, managing small groups, handling one-to-one review, giving feedback and making effective use of classroom assistants: in other words, all the skills of the good teacher, now clearly directed at maximising the achievement and progress of each pupil. It will involve a rigorous evaluation of the most effective ways of using IT to promote learning, for different groups of pupils. Attention will also have to be given to such practical issues as appropriate classroom layouts for different learning tasks. What is the basis for table groupings? Does the individual teacher control it, or should this, too, be a matter for more considered deliberation?

6.5 Conclusion: What Future for Differentiation?

In the last decade, which has seen so much change in schools, there has been a major shift in expectations about what all pupils should achieve during the period of statutory schooling, and indeed about what they probably can achieve. Repeated international comparisons, although not always valid or appropriate, have driven home the idea that the range of performance in this country is too wide; more specifically, that too many fail to reach recognised levels of competence. This is a not a new challenge; what has changed is the methods used to address it. Here differentiation has played an important part, and the development of thinking about, and application of, differentiation principles has mirrored broader changes in the approach to raising attainment.

In 1991, the team completing the national evaluation of the Lower Attaining Pupils' Programme decided it would be an enormous step forward to discuss the needs of the 'bottom 40 per cent' through the concept of differentiation for all pupils. At the start of the Programme, many planners and teachers had accepted, reluctantly or not, the idea of a 'lower attaining' minority for whom different goals, methods and, indeed, learning contexts were necessary. Drawing on the experience of schools in the Programme, it was possible to advocate the value of reviewing the learning needs of *all* pupils, since all had differing needs, related not only to 'ability' but to many other traits relevant to learning. Instead of hiving off some pupils into separate courses, fundamental questions could be asked about the quality of learning in the school as a whole, since the needs of 'lower attaining' pupils were not fundamentally different, and needed to be addressed throughout their time in the school if their attainment was to be raised.

In the intervening years, much has been achieved under the differentiation banner to raise awareness about learning needs and about a much wider range of strategies that can be used to improve learning and achievement. In particular, the contribution which learning support specialists can make, not only to helping teachers manage pupils with special educational needs more effectively but also to wider professional development in pedagogy, has been increasingly recognised by senior managers. By sharing their experience and expertise more fully within schools, primary teachers have demonstrated how much can be done to raise achievement by translating their knowledge of pupils into clear, challenging and appropriate learning targets. It is very important that these gains, often associated with initiatives for improving differentiation, are maintained.

But differentiation, as a strategy to support the raising of attainment, has had its downside too. There have been persistent difficulties of definition and confusions over the goal – whether this is to manage and permit increasingly differentiated outcomes or to encourage all to achieve higher levels through appropriately chosen methods, and perhaps over different time scales. It may be that the time has indeed come for a fresh terminology. What the new agenda of effective learning and target-setting offers is the possibility (no more) of turning the old dream into reality: that is, of raising attainment for *all* pupils. But no-one should underestimate the scale of the culture change which is required – for managers, teachers, pupils, teacher trainers, parents and the rest of the community.

REFERENCES

ADEY, P. and SHAYER, M. (1994). *Really Raising Standards: Cognitive Intervention and Academic Achievement.* London: Routledge.

AINSCOW, M. (Ed) (1989). *Special Education in Change.* London: David Fulton.

AINSCOW, M. (1994). *Special Needs in the Classroom: a teacher education guide.* London: Jessica Kingsley.

AINSCOW, M. (1998). 'Exploring links between special needs and school improvement', *Support for Learning*, **13**, 2, 70-5.

ALEXANDER R., ROSE, J., and WOODHEAD, C. (1992). *Curriculum Organisation and Classroom Practice in Primary Schools: a Discussion Paper.* London: DES.

BATES, B. and WOLTON, J. (1993). *Guidelines for Secondary Schools for Effective Differentiation in the Classroom.* Chelmsford: Essex County Council.

BEARNE, E. (Ed) (1996). *Differentiation and Diversity in the Primary School.* London: Routledge.

BROOKS, G. (1996). *Family Literacy Works: The NFER Evaluation of the Basic Skills Agency's Demonstration Programmes.* London: Basic Skills Agency.

BROWN, M. (Ed) (1992). *Graded Assessment in Mathematics (GAIM).* Walton-on-Thames: Nelson.

CAMBRIDGESHIRE COUNTY COUNCIL INSPECTORATE (1992). *Evaluation: Differentiated Learning. A Report by the Cambridgeshire Inspectorate.* Cambridge: Cambridgeshire County Council.

COOPER, P. and McINTYRE, D. (1996). *Effective Teaching and Learning: Teachers' and Students' Perspectives.* Buckingham: Open University Press.

DAVIDSON, B. and MOORE, J. (1996). 'Across the primary-secondary divide.' In: HART, S. (Ed) (1996). *Differentiation in the Secondary Curriculum: Debates and Dilemmas.* London: Routledge.

DEARING, SIR R. (1994). *The National Curriculum and Its Assessment: Final Report.* London: SCAA.

DEVON LOCAL EDUCATION AUTHORITY (1992). *A County Survey of Differentiation at Key Stage 3 in Devon.* Exeter: Devon LEA.

DICKINSON, C. and WRIGHT, J. (1993). *Differentiation: a Practical Handbook of Classroom Strategies.* Coventry: National Council for Educational Technology.

DODDINGTON, C. (1996). 'Grounds for differentiation: some values and principles in primary education considered.' In: BEARNE, E. (Ed) (1996). *Differentiation and Diversity in the Primary School.* London: Routledge.

EYRE, D. (1992). *Some Oxfordshire Secondary Schools' Approaches to More Able Pupils.* Oxford: Oxfordshire County Council Education Service.

EYRE, D. (1994). 'Differentiation and able pupils', *Flying High*, Spring, 27-32.

FOXMAN, D., HUTCHISON, D. and BLOOMFIELD, B. (1991). *The APU Experience 1977-1990.* London: School Examinations and Assessment Council.

GREAT BRITAIN. DEPARTMENT FOR EDUCATION AND EMPLOYMENT (1994). *Code of Practice on the Identification and Assessment of Special Educational Needs.* London: DFEE.

GREAT BRITAIN. DEPARTMENT FOR EDUCATION AND EMPLOYMENT. STANDARDS AND EFFECTIVENESS UNIT (1997). *From Targets to Action: Guidance to Support Effective Target-setting in Schools.* London: DFEE.

GREAT BRITAIN. DEPARTMENT OF EDUCATION AND SCIENCE. CENTRAL ADVISORY COUNCIL FOR EDUCATION (1967). *Children and their Primary Schools.* Plowden Report. London: HMSO.

GREAT BRITAIN. OFFICE FOR STANDARDS IN EDUCATION (1993). *Curriculum Organisation and Classroom Practice in Primary School: a Follow-up Report.* London: OFSTED.

GREAT BRITAIN. OFSTED. (1995a). *Guidance on the Inspection of Nursery and Primary Schools.* London: HMSO.

GREAT BRITAIN. OFSTED. (1995b). *Guidance on the Inspection of Secondary Schools.* London: HMSO.

GREAT BRITAIN. OFSTED. (1995c). *Guidance on the Inspection of Special Schools.* London: HMSO.

GREAT BRITAIN. OFSTED. (1995d). *Framework for the Inspection of Schools.* London: HMSO.

GREAT BRITAIN. OFSTED (1996). *Setting Targets to Raise Standards. An Introduction.* London: OFSTED.

GREAT BRITAIN. OFSTED and DEPARTMENT FOR EDUCATION AND EMPLOYMENT (1996). *Setting Targets to Raise Standards: A Survey of Good Practice.* London: DFEE.

GREAT BRITAIN. PARLIAMENT. HOUSE OF COMMONS (1997). *Excellence in Schools* (Cm. 3681). London: The Stationery Office.

GREAT BRITAIN. STATUTES (1993). *Education Act 1993, Chapter 35.* London: HMSO.

GROSS, J. (1993). *Special Educational Needs in the Primary School — a Practical Guide.* Buckingham: Open University Press.

HALL, S. (1997). 'The problem with differentiation', *School Science Review*, **78**, 284, 95-8.

HART, S. (1992). 'Differentiation. Part of the problem or part of the solution?', *The Curriculum Journal*, **3**, 2, 132-42.

HART, S. (Ed) (1996). *Differentiation in the Secondary Curriculum: Debates and Dilemmas.* London: Routledge.

HIASS, S. (1990). *Principles of Good Practice: a Tool for Self Evaluation.* Winchester: Hampshire County Council.

KENDALL, L. (1995). *Examination Results in Context. Report on the Analysis of the 1995 Examination Results.* London: Association of Metropolitan Authorities.

KERSHNER, R. and MILES, S. (1996). 'Thinking and talking about differentiation: "It's like a bar of soap…".' In: BEARNE, E. (Ed) (1996). *Differentiation and Diversity in the Primary School.* London: Routledge.

LEE, B., HARRIS, S. and DICKSON, P. (1995). *Continuity and Progression 5-16: Developments in Schools.* Slough: NFER.

McMGARVEY, B., MARRIOTT, S., MORGAN, V. and ABBOTT, L. (1997). 'Planning for differentiation: the experience of teachers in Northern Ireland primary schools', *Journal of Curriculum Studies*, **29**, 3, 351-63.

MORRIS, M. and TWITCHEN, R. (1990). *Evaluating Flexible Learning. A Users' Guide.* Slough: NFER.

NATIONAL COUNCIL FOR EDUCATIONAL TECHNOLOGY (1994). *Integrated Learning Systems: A Report of the Pilot Evaluation of Ils in the UK, January 1994 to July 1994.* Coventry: NCET.

NATIONAL COUNCIL FOR EDUCATIONAL TECHNOLOGY (1996). *Integrated Learning Systems: A Report on Phase II of the Pilot Evaluation of Ils in the UK.* Coventry: NCET.

NATIONAL FOUNDATION FOR EDUCATIONAL RESEARCH. (1997). *An Evaluation of the New Approach to the Initial Training of Careers Advisers. An Interim Study by NFER of the Initial Training Pilots Project.* Sheffield: Department for Education and Employment.

PETER, M. (Ed) (1992). 'Editorial to Special Issue on Differentiation', *British Journal of Special Education*, **19**, 1.

PETER, M. (Ed) (1994). *Differentiation: Ways Forward.* Stafford: The National Association for Special Educational Needs. (Reprinted from the *British Journal of Special Education*, **19**, 1, March 1992.)

POLLARD, A., BROADFOOT, P., CROLL, P., OSBORN, M. and ABBOTT, D. (1994). *Changing English Primary Schools? The Impact of the Education Reform Act at Key Stage One.* London: Cassell.

POSTLETHWAITE, K. (1993). *Differentiated Science Teaching: Responding to Individual Differences and to Special Educational Needs.* Buckingham: Open University Press.

QUALTER, A., McGUIGAN, L. and RUSSELL, T. (1995). 'Science department planning structures and their influence on the provision of differential teaching', *Evaluation and Research in Education*, **9**, 3, 149-61.

SAUNDERS, L. (1997). 'Value-added principles, practice and ethical considerations.' In: HARRIS, A. BENNETT, N. and PREDY, M. (Eds) *Organizational Effectiveness and Improvement in Education.* Buckingham: Open University Press.

SAUNDERS, L., STRADLING, B. and GALLACHER, S. (1996). *Raising Attainment in Secondary Schools: a Handbook for Self-evaluation.* Slough: NFER.

SCHAGEN, I. (1996). Quantitative Analysis for Self-Evaluation (QUASE). Technical Report. Analysis of GCSE Cohorts 1993-1995. Slough: NFER.

SCHAGEN, I. and WESTON, P. with HEWITT, D. and SIMS, D. (1997). *Hitting the Targets: Evaluation of Progress Towards Foundation Targets 1 and 3 by English Region.* Slough: NFER.

SCHAGEN, S. and KERR, D. (forthcoming) *Effective Progression from Primary to Secondary Schooling.* Slough: NFER.

SCHWEINHART, L.J. and WEIKART, D.P. (1997). *Lasting Differences: The High/Scope Preschool Curriculum Comparison Study Through Age 23.* Ypsilanti, Michigan: High/Scope Educational Research Foundation.

SCOTTISH OFFICE EDUCATION DEPARTMENT (1994). *Studies of Differentiation Practices in Primary and Secondary Schools* (Interchange 30). Edinburgh: SCRE.

SIMON, B. (1985). 'Imposing differentiation in schools', *Education Today and Tomorrow*, **37**, 3, 4-5.

SIMPSON, M. (Ed) (1989). *Differentiation in the Primary School: Classroom Perspectives.* Aberdeen: Northern College.

STRADLING, B. and SAUNDERS, L. (1993). 'Differentiation in practice: responding to the needs of all pupils', *Educational Research*, **35**, 2, 127-37.

STRADLING, R. and SAUNDERS, L. with WESTON, P. (1991). *Differentiation in Action: a Whole School Approach for Raising Attainment.* London: HMSO.

TAYLOR, M.J. (1996). 'Voicing their values: pupils' moral and cultural experience.' In: HALSTEAD, J.M and TAYLOR, M.J. (Eds) *Values in Education and Education in Values.* London: Falmer Press.

THORNDIKE, R., HAGEN, E. and FRANCE, N. (1996). (2 edn) *Cognitive Abilities Test (CAT).* Windsor: NFER-NELSON.

TOPPING, K.J. and WHITELEY, M. (1990). 'Participant evaluation of parent-tutored and peer-tutored projects in reading', *Journal of Educational Research*, **32**, 1, 14-32.

UNDERWOOD, J. and BROWN, J. (1997). *Integrated Learning Systems: Potential into Practice.* Oxford: Heinemann.

VISSER, J. (1993). *Differentiation: Making it Work. Ideas for Staff Development.* Stafford: NASEN Enterprises Ltd.

WESTON, P. (1988). *The Search for Success: an Overview of the Programme.* Slough: NFER.

WESTON, P. (1992). 'A decade for differentiation', *British Journal of Special Education*, **19**, 1, 6-9.

WILTSHIRE EDUCATION SUPPORT & TRAINING (1992). *Differentiating the Secondary Curriculum: Introduction and Guide to the Package.* Trowbridge: Wiltshire Education Support & Training (WEST).

APPENDIX: RESEARCH METHODS

The Project

The research presented in this report was carried out as part of the NFER's Membership Programme. This Programme is funded by the NFER's members, principally the LEAs of England and Wales. The research took place between October 1994 and December 1995. The aims of the project, as set out in the research summary, were to:

♦ review existing policies on differentiation at national, LEA and school levels;

♦ inform the ongoing debate on differentiation, progression and school effectiveness;

♦ evaluate the various strategies which primary and secondary schools are adopting in order to develop more effective differentiated teaching and learning. This will focus on different organisational strategies (e.g. pupil groupings); different management strategies for supporting and facilitating more effective differentiated teaching and learning; and differentiated classroom practice within specific subjects and across the whole curriculum.

The work fell into several stages, as set out below.

Stage 1. Exploratory

There were three main activities during this stage: a literature search, a telephone survey of LEAs and exploratory visits to schools.

The literature search was designed to identify published material in the UK relevant to differentiation, including books, articles and reports and to investigate the type of research findings and professional advice currently available to schools wanting to develop their differentiation policy.

The aim of the telephone survey was to find out how LEA advisers and inspectors with an interest in, or responsibility for, differentiation defined good practice in this area and what their LEA was doing to promote it, for example through staff development initiatives and practical support for schools. An additional purpose was to ask advisers/inspectors to help in suggesting schools which they felt were committed to their differentiation policy, and which we might approach for possible inclusion in the sample of case studies planned for the next stage of the research. The interviews were carried out between November 1994 and January 1995, using a semi-structured interview schedule. The aim was to telephone staff in half of the 116 LEAs in England and Wales at the time. In all, 70 advisers/inspectors were telephoned in 53 LEAs; some represented primary or secondary phases, some provided an overview of provision for the 5-16 age range.

Visits were made to a small number of primary and secondary schools known to the team and with a track record of commitment to differentiation. Each school was visited for a day, to trial early versions of interview and observation schedules and to test out ideas about differentiation practice emerging from the literature search and from our own earlier research.

Stage 2. Case Studies

A sampling frame of schools from which case study schools might be selected was drawn up, mainly on the basis of information supplied by the LEA staff in the telephone survey. Every effort was made to build up a balanced set of schools, representing both phases (primary and secondary), the main regions of England and Wales, and a range of socio-economic contexts. Attention was also paid to the approach to differentiation which the school appeared to have developed, so that a variety of approaches would be represented. Since the research programme would involve a number of visits and include classroom observation, it was important to obtain the goodwill of the head teacher and the staff at the outset.

As a result of these negotiations, four secondary schools, five primary schools and one special school took part in the first round of visits in the spring term of 1995. These visits were designed to obtain an overview of differentiation practice in the school, through interviews with staff, classroom observation, attendance at meetings and collection of documents. Staff interviews always included senior managers, subject leaders of the three core subjects of English, maths and science and the SENCO, and the classroom teachers whose lessons were observed. The programme was either completed in one session of two to three days or over two shorter visits.

During the summer and autumn terms of 1995, further visits were made, with two objectives in view. The first was to complete the common programme of work by extending the number of classroom observations and interviewing up to ten Key Stage 2 or Key Stage 3 pupils, chosen with staff advice to represent the range of ability in the school. For these interviews, a checklist of issues related to differentiation was used, to investigate their views on how far their individual learning needs were met, and what helped or hindered this process. The second objective was to explore particular issues or aspects of practice in each school that were relevant to the study. These included learning support strategies, individual programmes, progression from primary to secondary school and the use of laptop computers in class. For this second stage of the case-study programme two further secondary schools were included, to extend the range of practice, and in these schools the whole programme of interviews was completed during these two terms.

At the end of 1995, representatives of the case study schools were invited to a seminar at NFER to discuss their own approaches and some findings from the study. Finally, in November 1997, the head teachers of most of the case-study schools were telephoned to obtain an update on key features of their differentiation practice.

Stage 3. The National Survey

While the case studies had been selected to represent different approaches to differentiation and included schools in different geographical areas and socio-economic contexts, they were also by definition atypical because they had been identified by LEA staff as unusually committed to differentiation. We therefore wanted to know how far the views and practice of teachers and pupils in these schools were echoed in a random sample of schools across the country.

Self-completion postal questionnaires were designed, with questions based on concepts and findings that had emerged from the case studies. Parallel versions of the questionnaire were prepared for head teachers or other senior managers in primary and secondary schools. In addition, a shorter version was designed including questions of particular relevance to secondary heads of department in English, science and mathematics.

A national sample of 800 primary and 500 secondary schools was drawn from the NFER national database of schools. The survey was administered in the autumn term of 1995. All the primary schools in the sample were sent a single questionnaire. Secondary schools were sent one senior manager's questionnaire and one for each of the three heads of department. In all, 697 schools completed and returned the questionnaire, 405 primary schools and 292 secondary schools. Details of the response pattern are given in the table below.

Survey events		Primary schools	Secondary schools
1.	Initial sample numbers	800	500
2.	Withdrew from survey	4	9
3.	Questionnaires sent to	761	455
4.	Completed and returned	405	292
	Response rate (as % of (3))	53%	64%

Data from the questionnaires was coded, verified and entered by NFER staff and analysed by NFER statisticians led by the Chief Statistician, Dr Ian Schagen, in discussion with the rest of the research team. In addition to simple one- and two-way analyses, some variables were included in factor analyses and multiple regression analyses to identify underlying patterns and associations.